Praise for *Three Free Sins*

"*Three Free Sins* is a book that the world needs to read and Steve Brown is the only guy I know who is both Christian enough and irreligious enough to be able to have written it. My stepfather, Jack, once said, 'We don't need more people writing Christian books, what we need is more Christians writing good books,' and I agree with him. Steve has managed to write a good book that is also Christian—a rare achievement indeed. I have learned from it and enjoyed it at the same time, and you can't get better than that."

—Douglas Gresham, stepson of C. S. Lewis, author, speaker, *Chronicles of Narnia* producer

"As paradoxical as this may sound, if you are looking for a book that's fun to read and, at the same time, able to lead you into deep reflection on how the grace of God lifts the burdens of sin and guilt, you're going to love Steve Brown's book. He's not only a great communicator but a first rate theologian. I give this book four stars!"

—Tony Campolo, Ph.D., author of *Red Letter Christians*, professor emeritus, Eastern University, founder of the Evangelical Association for the Promotion of Education

"Steve Brown wholeheartedly believes that the gospel of grace is *way* more drastic, *way* more offensive, *way* more liberating, *way* more shocking, and *way* more counterintuitive than any of us realize. He understands at the deepest level that there is nothing more radically unbalanced and drastically unsafe than grace. It has no 'but': it's unconditional, uncontrollable, unpredictable, and undomesticated. It unsettles everything—and that's what this book will do to you. It will unsettle you. It will make you laugh, cry, rejoice, and scream. It will make you sad, glad, and mad, sometimes in the same paragraph! It will confront you and comfort you. Steve loves Jesus a lot, and this love shines brightly throughout this book. Everything here is vintage Steve Brown—the 'ole white guy at his best. Enjoy!"

—Tullian Tchividjian, pastor of Coral Ridge Presbyterian Church, author of *Jesus + Nothing = Everything*

"After reading Steve Brown's *Three Free Sins*, this rotten girl redeemed put on a pair of red stilettos and did a happy dance. *Three Free Sins* is like an old Three Dog Night tune—it'll make you sing along, crazy and loud, happy as all get-out. Steve Brown isn't the old bald guy he claims to be—he's all heart, graceful and true, and his message is indeed Joy to the World."

—Karen Spears Zacharias, author of *Will Jesus Buy Me a Double-Wide?*

"Once again Steve Brown has done what he does best. He's pushed the grace envelope. He's inviting us, no, *forcing* us to think through the radical implications of the gospel. As I read *Three Free Sins,* I got the clear impression that Steve wants us to take the command in 1 John 3:1 very seriously: 'See what great love the Father has lavished on us, that we should be called children of God!' 'Look, see, behold! God loves you so outrageously more than all you could ask or imagine, all because of what Jesus has done for you!' This book isn't about how the gospel gives us a grace card to live like moral morons, but as those who are radically transformed by the only love that will never let us go."

—Scotty Smith, founding pastor of Christ Community Church, author of *Objects of His Affection* and *Everyday Prayers*

"If Mark Twain had ever gotten over his cynicism long enough to believe the Gospel, he probably would have written a book like this. This is the kind of book that helps cynics like myself to actually hear the Gospel in the midst of all the social, religious, and political clap-trap that surrounds me. Thank God for friends and audacious preachers like Steve Brown. I am elated that he's still at it, to wit, upsetting the religious gatekeepers by throwing open the Gospel door so that all the riff-raff like me can actually see inside. Wow, there's a party going on! Who woulda thought?"

—Buddy Greene, singer-songwriter, entertainer, recording artist

"Steve Brown hates self-help books. Thank God. *Three Free Sins* is hilarious, honest, and full of the hard-won wisdom only an old guy knows. At its core is this truth: real change only happens when we realize God loves us whether we change or not. Do you know that in your knower? Read this book. It won't self-help you into frustration. It will change your game. And if you are like me, you'll laugh out loud, cry a little, and shout, 'Amen! Preach it, Old White Guy!'"

—Susan E. Isaacs, author of *Angry Conversations with God*

Three Free Sins

GOD'S NOT MAD AT YOU

STEVE BROWN

HOWARD BOOKS
A DIVISION OF SIMON & SCHUSTER, INC.
New York · Nashville · London · Toronto · Sydney · New Delhi

Ħ
Howard Books
A Division of Simon & Schuster, Inc.
1230 Avenue of the Americas
New York, NY 10020

First Howard Books trade paperback edition February 2012

HOWARD and colophon are trademarks of Simon & Schuster, Inc.

For information about special discounts for bulk purchases, please contact Simon
& Schuster Special Sales at 1-866-506-1949 or business@simonandschuster.com.

The Simon & Schuster Speakers Bureau can bring authors to your live event. For
more information or to book an event contact the Simon & Schuster Speakers
Bureau at 1-866-248-3049 or visit our website at www.simonspeakers.com.

Designed by Helene Berinsky

Manufactured in the United States of America

10   9   8   7   6   5   4   3

Library of Congress Cataloging-in-Publication Data

Brown, Stephen W.
Three free sins: god's not mad at you / Steve Brown.
p.   cm.
Includes bibliographical references.
1. Grace (Theology)   2. Sin—Christianity.   I. Title.   II. Title: Three free sins.
BT761.3.B76 2012
234—dc23
2011023306

ISBN 978-1-4516-1226-4
ISBN 978-1-4516-1230-1 (ebook)

To my friend "J"

who struggles with HIV, guilt, and grace . . .

. . . and whose struggle, authenticity, and perseverance

make this "cynical old preacher" less cynical.

CONTENTS

INTRODUCTION

Not too long ago I decided to offer three free sins to all Christian callers to my syndicated talk show, *Steve Brown Etc*. Six, if they called from a cell phone.

That's right: free sins.

Not everyone was thrilled with the offer.

ME: You're on the air.

CALLER: I'm angry . . . really angry!

ME: Okay. What's making you angry?

CALLER: It's this three free sins thing. It's not right!

ME: Alright, I'll give you four.

CALLER: You don't understand. This is not funny!

ME: Okay, I'll give you five . . . but that's as high as I'm going.

CALLER: This is blasphemous! And you're hurting the cause of Christ![1]

ERIK (the producer): Lady, chill out. Steve can't give you free sins. It's a joke!

We receive thousands of letters, emails, and phone calls at Key Life each month, and a significant portion of those who write or call are upset with something they have read, heard, or seen at one of Key Life's various ministry efforts. More than a few people responded in anger at my offer of three free sins.

"You are encouraging sin. Repent!"
"I will never listen to you again!"
"I don't think you're even saved."
"I'm deeply offended by what you teach. Jesus is too!"

So why am I writing a book about it? Maybe I'm crazy.

When Barry Goldwater ran for president, he went to Florida and spoke against Social Security; to Tennessee and spoke against the TVA; to Washington and railed against politics. One of his Senate friends said to him, "Barry, there's an angry bull in that field. Now, I know you have to go through the field, but do you have to wave a red flag at him every time you do?"

Maybe you picked up this book because you were intrigued with the title. Maybe you are a sinner looking for a pass. Could be that you're a committed Christian and just can't understand how a Christian book could be this off-base. Perhaps you're on a heresy hunt.

I do suspect, however, that no matter why you picked up this book, you have a question for me: *Why in the world would you write a book like this? Do you really think it's smart to wave a red flag at that bull?*

All my life I've struggled, with very little success, to stay within the "religious box." Most of the time I've ended up offending people I didn't mean to offend and saying things that seemed true and biblical only to find out that a lot of people, many of whom I deeply respect, disagreed. A number of years ago, an elderly lady called a talk show in Dallas where I was the guest. She was a delight and said, "Steve, if people could see beyond your nonsense to your heart, they would really like you."

But make no mistake: this book isn't nonsense for you to see beyond. I really mean this free-sins business. So much so that one of my friends recently told me,

> *All my life I've struggled, with very little success, to stay within the "religious box."*

"You've really done it! You're going to lose your job, be kicked out of the church, fired from the seminary where you teach, and offend the friends and supporters you've got left. Why would you write a book like this?"

I'm doing it because I just can't help it.

I've always been impressed and moved by the words of Martin Luther at the Diet of Worms in 1521 when he was asked to either renounce or reaffirm his writings. He said, "Unless I am convinced by proofs from Scriptures or by plain and clear reasons and arguments, I can and will not retract, for it is neither safe nor wise to do anything against conscience. Here I stand. I can do no other. God help me. Amen."

I know, I know. I'm no Martin Luther. But I do think I understand what he felt. Sometimes you want to run, but you can't. Sometimes you think it's insane that you're saying what you're saying, but you just can't shut up. Sometimes you want to say things that are acceptable and pleasing, but the truth keeps getting in the way . . . and once you've seen truth, you can't unsee it.

Besides that, I really do care. For years I pretended that I didn't. I would say to people that I wasn't their mother, that I was not responsible for them, and that they should talk to someone who cared. But it was a smoke screen. I knew that if I cared (or admitted I cared), my caring would fill my dreams and ruin my life.

But, God help me, I really do care.

I care about the church. I care about the thousands of people who are part of the church and who have told me about their sins, their failures, their fears, and their loneliness. I care about those who are running away from God and those who never came to him in the first place because he was so big and scary. I care about the leaders in the church who are sure God is angry and would give anything to know that he isn't. I care about the people who get the truth right but never apply it to themselves. I care about sinners who can't believe that God could ever like them. I care about those whose secrets are making them sick, whose guilt is making them neurotic, and whose fear prevents any kind of remedy. I care about people who have forgotten how to dance and laugh because dancing and laughing are unseemly and might not please a holy God.

But it's more than that. I can never speak as an outsider of the human race. I wear the same T-shirt.

> *I care about people who have forgotten how to dance and laugh because dancing and laughing are unseemly and might not please a holy God.*

Too many books are written by experts sharing their expertise. This is not one of them.

This book is a witness. It's a witness to the eternal verities of the Christian faith, to the surprising discovery that God isn't angry at his people, and to the incredible wholeness that comes when one encounters the *real* God . . . not the one "they" told us about.

This book is simply the words of one needy, fearful, sinful, confused, and joyous beggar telling other beggars where he found bread.

I often say at the end of my sermons, "Fifty percent of what I just taught you is wrong. I'm just not sure which fifty percent. So, you're going to have to get your Bible and do some checking."

That drives Christians nuts because we're all looking for someone to follow who has all the answers and is willing to lead. I'm not that person. I used to be, but I've repented.

So I'm writing this book because I can't help it. It may make you angry. You might read it and think that nothing could be this good. Perhaps you, like me, have a heart that is sometimes tired, sometimes cynical, and is weary of playing the religious game. It could be that you'll want to check with the experts about what I've written. You may be longing for hope and think maybe you'll find a bit here.

Or it could be that after you read this book, you'll end up burning it.

Whatever.

My friend Dan Allender spoke at one of our pastors' conferences and said, "The Christian faith and the grace at its heart is so radical that most congregations can't deal with it. So you have to parcel it out little bits at a time . . . until you get the kids through college."

Well, my kids are through college, and I'm an old white guy. There isn't any leverage on me anymore. I don't need a job, I'm not trying to climb the career ladder, I'm happy with the woman I'm married to, and I don't want anything from anybody but Jesus.

But still, truth be told, I would rather not write this book. In fact, I wouldn't do this for anybody but Jesus.

So let's begin.

I know that nothing good dwells in me, that is, in my flesh.

For I have the desire to do what is right,

but not the ability to carry it out.

For I do not do the good I want,

but the evil I do not want is what I keep on doing.

—Romans 7:18–19

1

. . .

The Impossible Task of Flying Frogs

Someone recently sent me a statement purported to be from a public school teacher who was applying for a position in the school system:

> Let me see if I've got this right: You want me to go into that room with those kids, correct their disruptive behavior, observe them for signs of abuse, monitor their dress habits, censor their T-shirt messages, and instill in them a love for learning. You want me to check their backpacks for weapons, wage war on drugs and sexually transmitted diseases, and raise their sense of self-esteem and personal pride. You want me to teach them patriotism and good citizenship, sportsmanship and fair play, and how to register to vote, balance a checkbook, and apply for a job. You want me to check their heads for lice, recognize signs of antisocial behav-

ior, and make sure that they all pass the state exams. You want me to provide them with an equal education regardless of their handicaps, and communicate regularly with their parents by letter, telephone, newsletter, and report cards. You want me to do all of this with a starting salary that qualifies me for food stamps . . .

. . . and then you tell me I can't pray?

Now that's not a great job! But I can top it! I've had a lousy job for most of my life!

I'm a preacher/pastor, and my job description is to keep people from doing what they obviously want to do. I've often felt like a police officer at a rock concert charged with keeping the concertgoers from smoking pot. Everywhere I turn, people are lighting up, and the air is so sweet that I feel like a mosquito in a nudist colony.

With a job description like mine, I hardly ever get invited to parties (at least, not the good ones). Sometimes I feel like a wet shaggy dog shaking himself at a wedding. I tell the guests that I'm trying to help and that God anointed me to reach out to them, but they simply don't care.

Preachers are supposed to keep people from sinning. I haven't been very successful so far. And I've been trying for forty years.

There are times when I feel like I'm standing by the sheer edge of a high cliff that people frequently approach. "Be careful," I tell them. "It's a long way down and coming to a stop at the bottom will be quite unpleasant." They look at me. They sometimes even thank me.

Then they jump.

But I keep at it. "Hey," I say to the next group who approach the cliff, "not too long ago, I saw people go off that cliff; if you'll bend over

> *They look at me. They sometimes even thank me. Then they jump.*

and look, you can see the bloody mess they made." Like everybody else, they seem grateful for my concern. They may even say something about my compassion and wisdom.

Then they jump. It happens again and again.

Frankly, I'm tired of it. In fact, I've given up standing by this stupid cliff. I'm tired of being people's mother. I'm tired of trying to prevent the unpreventable. I'm tired of talking to people who don't want to listen. And I'm tired of pointing out the obvious.

Just when I determine to leave my position by the cliff, to my horror and surprise . . .

I jump!

What's with that?

Let me tell you. Human beings have an undeniable proclivity to sin—to jump off the cliff. We're drawn to it. We love it (at least for a while). No matter who tries to keep us from doing it or how much pain it will cause, we are irresistibly drawn to that cliff. Maybe we want to fly. Could it be that we have a masochistic streak in our DNA?

Could it be that our default position is jumping off cliffs? I don't know. But for whatever reason, we do jump, we do get hurt, and—if we survive—we then climb back up the cliff and jump again.

I heard a parable (author unknown) about Felix the flying frog. Even though it mixes the metaphor a bit, let me tell it to you.

Once upon a time, there lived a man named Clarence who had a pet frog named Felix. Clarence lived a modestly comfortable existence on what he earned working at the Walmart, but he always dreamed of being rich. "Felix!" he said one day, hit by sudden inspiration, "We're going to be rich! I'm going to teach you to fly!"

Felix, of course, was terrified at the prospect. "I can't fly, you twit! I'm a frog, not a canary!"

Clarence, disappointed at the initial response, told Felix: "That negative attitude of yours could be a real problem. We're going to remain poor, and it will be your fault."

So Felix and Clarence began their work on flying.

On the first day of the "flying lessons," Clarence could barely control his excitement (and Felix could barely control his bladder). Clarence explained that their apartment building had fifteen floors, and each day Felix would jump out of a window, starting with the first floor and eventually getting to the top floor.

After each jump, they would analyze how well he flew, isolate the most effective flying techniques, and implement the improved process for the next flight. By the time they reached the top floor, Felix would surely be able to fly.

Felix pleaded for his life, but his pleas fell on deaf ears. *He just doesn't understand how important this is,* thought Clarence. *He can't see the big picture.*

So, with that, Clarence opened the first-floor window and threw Felix out. He landed with a thud.

The next day, poised for his second flying lesson, Felix again begged not to be thrown out of the window. Clarence told Felix about how one must always expect resistance when introducing new, innovative plans.

With that, he threw Felix out the second-story window. THUD!

Now this is not to say that Felix wasn't trying his best. On the fifth day, he flapped his legs madly in a vain attempt at flying. On the sixth day, he tied a small red cape around his neck and tried to think Superman thoughts. It didn't help.

By the seventh day, Felix, accepting his fate, no longer begged for mercy. He simply looked at Clarence and said, "You know you're killing me, don't you?"

Clarence pointed out that Felix's performance so far had been less than exemplary, failing to meet any of the milestone goals he had set for him.

With that, Felix said quietly, "Shut up and open the

window," and he leaped out, taking careful aim at the large jagged rock by the corner of the building.

Felix went to that great lily pad in the sky.

Clarence was extremely upset, as his project had failed to meet a single objective that he had set out to accomplish. Felix had not only failed to fly, he hadn't even learned to steer his fall as he dropped like a sack of cement, nor had he heeded Clarence's advice to "fall smarter, not harder."

The only thing left for Clarence to do was to analyze the process and try to determine where it had gone wrong. After much thought, Clarence smiled and said . . .

"Next time, I'm getting a smarter frog!"

A number of years ago, I realized that I was, as it were, trying to teach frogs to fly. Frogs can't fly. Not only that, they get angry when you try to teach them. The gullible ones will try, but they eventually get hurt so bad, even they quit trying. And let me tell you a secret: the really sad thing about being a "frog flying teacher" is that I can't fly either.

If you are a teacher trying to teach frogs to fly, nobody ever bothers to ask if *you* can fly. In fact, if you pretend that you're an expert and tell a lot of stories about flying; if you can throw in a bit of aeronautical jargon about stalls, spins, and flight maneuvers; and if you carry around a flying manual and know your way around it, nobody will question your ability to fly. You just pretend you're an expert, and the students think you can fly.[1]

For years, as a preacher charged with preventing people from sinning, that was my problem (and sometimes it still is). I became so phony I could hardly stand myself.

> If you are a teacher trying to teach frogs to fly, nobody ever bothers to ask if you can fly.

I know, I know, there is a lot more to being a preacher and a pastor than keeping people from sinning, but if you become obsessed with sin prevention, it begins to take over everything you do and teach. Pretty soon you become a police officer, and the crime is sin. You spend your time trying to discern what is and what isn't sin, you emphasize "sin prevention" by teaching how to avoid sin and stay pure, and you create a disciplinary process whereby sin is punished in the name of Jesus and "for their own good."

PULLING BACK THE CURTAIN

Have you ever watched the television program that reveals the secrets of magicians? It's called *Magic's Biggest Secrets Revealed*. If you've seen it, you know there is this weird, masked man who looks kind of scary. He does the impossible, to wit, performs major illusions to the astonishment of the audience. And then after the trick is demonstrated, he goes back and step-by-step reveals how he did it.

I suspect that professional magicians are not altogether happy with this television show. It's kind of like the Wizard of Oz who is big and scary . . . until Toto pulls the curtain aside. Everybody then sees that behind the big, scary, demanding image on the screen is a little man pulling levers. I hardly ever go to magic shows anymore. I used to love seeing the illusions and being astonished by an illusionist who did things that seemed impossible. I just don't enjoy them anymore. The television show took the fun out of it, and I wish I had never watched it.

With my apologies to the teachers of flying frogs (i.e., preachers and teachers), I'm going to pull back the curtain and tell you how I did it—and sometimes still do. It's a problem, you know? If you can't fly and have been charged with teaching others how to fly—who also can't and never will be able to fly—you have to be very good at creating a facade. And not only that, the problem is compounded when you believe that the master flyer (God) has commissioned you to do it.

Being a preacher and a pastor is like that. And it will kill you if you let it. Trying to teach people not to sin and, at the same time, finding out that they are still sinning is not a fulfilling task. Neither is trying to cover up that you have your own sins too (maybe bigger than your students'/parishioners').

Let me give you some of the techniques of teaching frogs to fly and of keeping people from sinning.

1. Manipulate with guilt.

You would be surprised at how far a "How could you?" or "After all that Jesus has done for you!" will go if it is said with sincerity and passion. It's even better and more effective if you can attach a Bible verse to it.

Last week I heard about a preacher who said that heaven wasn't going to be a happy place for some Christians. "When you look back and see how many opportunities you missed and how often you failed when you could have succeeded, it will be depressing." Now that's over the top. Okay, okay, I did some guilt manipulation over the years, but at least I left heaven alone. It's almost like this preacher is not content with making people miserable on earth. He has to mess with heaven too.

2. "Encourage" with comparisons to how much better others have done.

It's sort of like the rooster who found a gigantic eagle's egg. He rolled it into the chicken coop and said, "Ladies, I don't want you to think I'm complaining, but I did want you to know what the competition is doing."

3. Tell stories of heroes of the faith who persevered and were faithful in the hard places.

"If they can do it, God will give you the grace to do it too!" It's very important that, when motivating with biography, you not tell the whole story. You have to leave out the sin, the doubts, and the failures. Only reference the victories.

4. Use the carrot-and-stick technique.

This is one of the best techniques there is. The carrot is heaven, of course, and the stick is hell. After someone becomes a Christian, the hell thing doesn't work very well, but there is always Hebrews 12:8 ("If you are left without discipline, in which all have participated, then you are illegitimate children and not sons"). It's a simple matter of telling your congregation that while they probably won't go to hell for their sins, God will break their legs if they get out of line. A few attention-grabbing words like "cancer," "financial ruin," and "leprosy" help.

5. Throw out the "follow me as I follow Christ" thing.

The trick here is to never let them see you sweat. You have to look spiritual, speak spiritual, and act spiritual when people are around. If they catch you in an unguarded moment, the gig is up. But it's doable. I was able to pull it off for a whole lot of years.

• • •

The above list is, of course, truncated. For a price, I can send you a complete manual on keeping people from sinning. I have, however, given you enough so you get the idea.

Now, can we talk?

That stuff is sick. And that's our problem, the problem I want to address for the next few chapters.

Simply put, we're in serious trouble in the church. It isn't because we are sinners or because we don't know enough, pray enough, or read the Bible enough. Our problem isn't about being more faithful or not living a supernatural life of victory. Our problem isn't going to be fixed with more programs, better methods of evangelism and stewardship, or discipline. Our problem isn't spiritual formation or that we aren't missional.

Our problem is that we have taken the best news ever given to the world, run it through a "religious" grid, and made something unpalatable out of it. In short, we've taken the good

> *We have taken the best news ever given to the world, run it through a "religious" grid, and made something unpalatable out of it.*

news and made it bad news. And if you listen carefully, you can hear old Slew Foot (that would be the devil) laughing.

WHAT IF THE CHRISTIAN FAITH ISN'T ABOUT GETTING BETTER?

So, what if you had three free sins?

Better, what if you had unlimited free sins? Even better yet, what if your sins weren't even the issue? What if the issue were living your life with someone who loved you without condition or condemnation?

What if the Christian faith wasn't about getting better at all?

I have a friend who is struggling with HIV. He was raised in a "Christian" atmosphere of condemnation. I'll tell you more about "J" in a later chapter, but for now, you need to know that he is just "hanging on." My friend sinned and the light went out. He thought God turned it out, sure that he had received what he deserved and that God was punishing him with HIV. He thought God said, "I've had it with you."

I told "J" that Jesus wasn't surprised or angry. He has reached out to Jesus very hesitantly. He told me not too long ago that he would run, but he had no place to go. Good.

I'm glad my friend with HIV is hanging on because I'm writing this book for him. He's come to a place where he doesn't much like the Christian faith he has been taught, but it's the only game in town.

Maybe you're where "J" is.

On the other hand, maybe you just can't do it anymore. Maybe you are fed up with the games and the failed efforts and have decided not to do it anymore. Maybe you just gave up and left. I have another friend who did just that.

One of my favorite sounds is the sound of motorcycles in the morning. I know that's strange, and frankly, I haven't always liked that sound. At the beginning, it was a horrible sound—but not because it was loud or because I don't like motorcycles. It was a horrible sound because it was the sound of leaving.

He was a staff member in a major drug-rehabilitation ministry where the boundaries and rules were very strict and violation of those rules exacted a stiff penalty. Being on the staff, he was the enforcer.

He stopped by my study at the church where I was the pastor and said, "The only reason I'm here is because I didn't want you to hear it from someone else. I've resigned, because I can't do it anymore. I'm headed for Key West, and I'm going there to sin. I may never come back. If there is a God, He's going to have to bring me back; and if there isn't a God, you won't see me again."

I had a lot of things to say to him, but he wouldn't let me say them. He told me that he already knew what I was going to say and not to say it. So I watched him leave my study, go out into the parking lot, and head south on his motorcycle. It was a sad sound—the sound of that motorcycle. For the next three months, I prayed for my friend, and sometimes if I thought about it much, the tears would well up in my eyes.

Then I heard the sound again. I heard the sound of a motorcycle pulling into the church parking lot. My "prodigal" friend was grinning. "I thought you would want to know," he said, laughing. "There really is a God and I'm back."

Even as I tell you about that morning, I want to shout and laugh.

So read the rest of this book and you'll never be able to say, "Nobody ever told me."

There was a time when Wittenberg, the town where Martin Luther served, went crazy. As the doctrines taught by Luther took root, so did a lot of weird behavior and not a little sin. Luther was depressed, and a friend asked him if he had to do it over again, would he have preached the same gospel of grace?

Luther thought for a moment and said that he would do the same thing because it would be better for them to know the gospel and not live it, than not to know the gospel.

Luther knew what I know about the message of God's grace. If you "get it," you will always come back.

And when you do, it will be as if you never left.

I find it to be a law that when I want to do right,

evil lies close at hand.

For I delight in the law of God, in my inner being,

but I see in my members another law waging war

against the law of my mind and making me captive

to the law of sin that dwells in my members.

Wretched man that I am!

Who will deliver me from this body of death?

—Romans 7:21–24

2
• • •

How's It Working for You So Far?

Let me ask you a question. I won't embarrass or shame you, but you really do need to find an answer. The question is this: How's it working for you so far?

I once spoke at a prominent Christian conference center. All I had to do was speak once each morning and enjoy the place the rest of the time. There were evening concerts, great food, and a magnificent natural setting with a large lake, camping grounds, and a hotel. I loved it!

That is, until I got caught smoking my pipe in my room.

Evidently that wasn't done. In fact, I think the powers that be decided I probably wasn't even saved. The maid put a sign up in my room to remind me that no smoking was allowed and suggest that if I did it again, I would get the fever and die. They didn't send me home, but it was clear they wanted to. It would be difficult, I suppose, to explain why the main speaker at a large conference was sent packing.

I, of course, put my pipe away for Jesus' sake and continued to speak each morning for the conference. They had assigned me a topic—The Cross of Christ. This was a rather narrow and orthodox Christian conference, so I remained carefully "within the box" of orthodoxy. (Contrary to what some people believe about me, that wasn't hard given that my convictions and worldview are narrow and orthodox.)

However, orthodoxy can be about as exciting as a bag of chicken feet if it isn't applied to the reality of living . . . and applied as radically as orthodoxy is. Up until that Wednesday morning, I was straight, conservative, orthodox, and boring. In fact, my teaching sessions reminded me of someone reading from John Calvin's *Institutes* or Louis Berkhof's *Systematic Theology*. (Those are great works in a flood . . . you can stand on them and stay perfectly dry!) Frankly, we were all bored out of our skulls and nobody would admit it.

That is when I decided to "go out in a blaze of glory."

The powers were already unhappy with me. If they were looking for an excuse to send me home, I wanted it to be for something bigger than smoking a fine briar with expensive and pleasant-smelling tobacco. So, in that morning session, I closed my notes on the theology of the cross and said, "Can we talk?"

This conference took place, by the way, shortly after I

had resigned as the pastor of a church I had served for almost twenty years. I won't bore you with the details, but the short version is that the wheels were coming off my wagon. Nobody knew it (I managed to keep up a good front), but I was very close to burnout and resigned to discover what was driving me. During that first year, I discovered all kinds of things about me that weren't altogether pleasant, but which were quite revealing (for example, what it means to be the adult child of an alcoholic, how I had become the world's mother, why I was so afraid of letting anybody get close, and why I was so insecure and afraid).

In that period of time, the cross of Christ became far more to me than a theological construct to be taught and defended. The cross became the focal point of my hope for health and wholeness.

> I won't bore you with the details, but the short version is that the wheels were coming off my wagon.

TELLING SECRETS

So in this conference session, I decided to take off the armor and "get down." I talked about my grandfather's suicide, about my father being the son of a single mother (making me a second-generation bastard), about confronting my father's mistress when I was so young I didn't even know what a mistress was, and about always feeling that I was on the outside looking in. I talked about my fear of abandonment and the dark nights when my mother threatened to leave. I referenced my fear of failure and my desire to control.

In other words, I decided to tell my secrets and then to talk about how the cross began to cover, heal, and free me. I talked about forgiveness, sin, and love in a highly personal and improper way. Looking back, I suspect that some of the things I said were rather shocking. And I fully expected to be stoned.

Just the opposite happened. The response of those dear people was incredibly surprising. I've never seen so many people that quiet for that long. Then people started taking out their handkerchiefs and wiping their eyes.

When I finished teaching and exited the platform, I stood waiting to see if anybody wanted to talk. I looked to my left and saw a very big, angry-looking man rushing down the aisle toward me. I thought he was going to kill me and prepared to die. When he raised his arms to hit me, to my surprise he hugged me instead, picking me up off the ground. That's when I noticed he was crying. "Steve," he said, "my father committed suicide, and I've never told anybody that before."

When he finally put me down, I turned around, and a woman was standing beside me in great distress. "Steve, I need to talk to you. I was sexually abused as a child, and I've got to tell someone." Another man told me that both his parents were drunks and that he had spent most of his life denying it to himself and to everybody else. The confessions were so numerous that even I was shocked. It went on and on. In fact, so many people told me their secrets and stories that the rest of the week I hardly had time to eat at meals.

What happened? Someone (that would be me) noticed that the "emperor (that would be us) was buck naked" and said so. Someone questioned the rubric of being nice and proper. Someone pointed out that there was a bad smell in the room that we'd tried to cover with "religious perfume."

For some reason, people tell me their secrets. I don't solicit the secrets and often don't know what to do with them. I sometimes even wish people wouldn't tell them to me. They continue to tell me their secrets not because I'm so wise or know so much. And I don't think it's because they think I can "pass a miracle." Perhaps when you have a deep and authoritative voice (I do) and you're old (I'm as old as dirt), people kind of think of you as a Yoda figure. It could be that really needy people only feel comfortable telling their secrets to other needy people. It might be that I'm fairly unconditional. After all, when a person has as many sins and secrets as I do, he or she doesn't throw many rocks. But for whatever reason, all kinds of people tell me their secrets.

Frederick Buechner (the American writer and theologian), among others, has said that when we tell our secrets to someone else or even to ourselves, those secrets lose their power. I have a friend who says that one must "kiss the demons [of our lives] on the lips" before they can be "defanged."

When people tell me their secrets, my response is often: "So? You thought that Jesus didn't have to die for you? You thought that God sent a rule book and told you to follow it or else? You thought you surprised a God who had perspiration on his upper lip and high hopes for your success? You thought you could speak as an outsider of the human race?"

The response I mostly get is one of surprise and relief.

When was the last time that surprise and relief were your reactions to God? In other words, how's it working for you so far?

If you're not much of a believer—and consider yourself just "religious" or "spiritual"—the question is either irrelevant or quite disturbing. If you're fine so far (that's what the man said who jumped off a twenty-story building as he passed the fifteenth story), if you don't feel much need to change, and if you're fairly content, I'm glad for you. This is not a book for you. But if things go south, do call and I'll do what I can.

If you're a Christian, things are fine, and you're living "the victorious Christian life," I'm happy for you too. You're part of my family, and I always rejoice when family members do well. But I don't think you're going to like this book very much either, so you might as well stop reading it right now. (If you haven't marked it up, you may be able to take it back to the store and get your money back.)

If things should go south for you, you can call, too, and I'll do what I can.

HAVE YOU HAD IT WITH THE PAYBACK PAIN?

In our "Born Free" seminar at Key Life, we teach a principle about how change takes place. The principle is this: *Real change doesn't take place until the pain gets greater than the payback.*

In other words, almost everything we do, believe, and think has a payback attached to it. People are, for instance, rarely "good for goodness' sake." They are good because there is usually a payback. Conversely, people are rarely evil for evil's sake. There is a payback in that instance too. In fact, this book is only for those who are worn out by religious promises that don't deliver, goodness that can't be realized, and faithfulness that doesn't make it. If you're there and you've had it with the payback pain, I've got some things to say that I think will be helpful . . . maybe even change your life.

First, though, you have to face the pain, own it, and make it teach you important stuff. I have a friend who, after an injury, went through weeks of physical therapy. He told me that he had learned the secret of physical therapy, to wit, find out where it hurts and probe it to make it hurt more. Eventually, if the therapist hurts you enough, you will get well. My friend, Larry Crabb, the Christian psychologist, says something like that about emotional pain. When it hurts, don't run. Go there and probe it until it hurts so bad that only Jesus can fix it.

Do you ever wonder why people continue with destructive and painful behavior when they know it is destructive and painful? It's because, even if they can't see it, there is a payback for that behavior.

Jesus once asked a sick man if he wanted to be healed. The man had been sick for thirty-eight years, and the question seemed ridiculous. Want to be healed? The man must have looked at Jesus as if Jesus had lost his mind.

But when you think about it, it was a wise question. Jesus knew the man didn't have to wash the dishes or take the trash out. He got a whole lot of sympathy and I suspect even admiration. He didn't have to worry about failure because nobody expects a crippled man to succeed. He could just moan and everybody got concerned. Jesus knew all of that.

There is an insightful scene in Calvin Miller's *The Singer.* The Singer encounters a miller who has a deformed hand. Years before, his hand had been caught in the grinder of the mill at harvest time. The Singer offers to make him whole with his healing melody, and the miller says that the Singer is mocking him. In fact, the miller says that the Singer is making it worse by calling attention to the malady. The miller then falls on the floor in pain. "He waited for the Singer to join him in his pity, but when he raised his head for understanding, the door stood open on the night and the Singer was nowhere to be seen."[1]

Do you ever feel that Jesus "is nowhere to be seen"?

Most of us remember the promises. There were a lot of them. We were told that we would be free from guilt and condemnation. We ran to the church, thinking that finally we had found family who loved and supported one another. We were taught about the providence of God, the joyful process of sanctification, and the return of Christ, who would clean up whatever mess was left. We sang, "The cross before us, the world behind us. No turning back. No turning back." We meant it when we sang it. And we told everyone who would listen.

For most of us that was a long time ago. Since then, some railed against the church, Jesus, and anything religious. I get that. Some gave up and quietly left. Some still hang around the church, but it feels like a den of porcupines. It's simply not true that "every day in every way, I am getting better and better."[2] And we are all so very afraid and guilty. To make matters worse, we don't tell one another the truth because it violates the rules of the game. So we just fake it.

TRYING TO MAKE THINGS BETTER
ALMOST ALWAYS MAKES THEM WORSE

Now let me give you a truth that can make all the difference in the world: almost everything you think about doing to make something better is wrong and will only make that something worse. Trust me. I've been there often and tried it all. I'm trying to save you a lot of hassle and pain.

Teenagers think I'm very wise. I'm not. After years of watching, I know how human relationships work. When teenagers are devastated over the loss of their boyfriends or girlfriends, I tell them, "If you do exactly what I tell you, you'll get another chance. First, everything that 'feels' right is wrong, and everything you don't think you should do is probably exactly what you should do. Don't beg and don't let them see you sweat; instead, let them think you're fine and are looking for someone else. Don't call. Don't write. Don't make promises, and whatever you do, don't stalk. Stay the course and you'll get another shot."

They do, and when they get the second chance, they are amazed that the old white guy is that smart.

It's the same way with us and our emptiness, guilt, and fear. Almost everything we've been taught to do and think is not only wrong, it only makes things worse. Trying harder doesn't work. You should know that by now. Becoming more religious will only magnify the problem. Being disciplined and making a commitment will, more often than not, cause you to "hit the rocks of reality"; and your efforts, in the end, will turn to dust. Pretending is stupid. At some point, you will slip up and be shamed. And reading the latest book on making an impact, changing your world, or being driven by a purpose (as good as those things can be) will probably drive you nuts. You will only feel guiltier. Motivational advice, biblical directives, challenges, and resolutions are dogs that simply won't hunt anymore.

John Newton (the writer of "Amazing Grace") said this: "The gracious purposes to which the Lord makes the sense and feeling of our depravity subservient, are manifold.

> *Almost everything we've been taught to do and think is not only wrong, it only makes things worse.*

Hereby his own power, wisdom, faithfulness and love, are more signally displayed: his power, in maintaining his own work in the midst of so much opposition, like a spark burning in the water, or a bush unconsumed in the flames; his wisdom, in defeating and controlling all the devices which Satan, from his knowledge of the evil of our nature, is encouraged to practise against us."[3]

So now what? Should I just give up?

Yeah!

Well, maybe not give up, but something that certainly feels like giving up.

THERE'S A LOT TO BE SAID FOR SELF-RIGHTEOUSNESS

Self-righteousness is just another name for self-sufficiency. It is a horrible trait for a number of reasons. First, it is always a lie. Nobody is that righteous, and hardly anybody is that sufficient. Second, it requires a mask. And if we wear that mask long enough, it will make us phony and empty. Third, it will cause others to label us "hypocrites." If people don't know us, it will cause them to either run in the opposite direction or become as sick as we are.

But more important than anything else, self-righteousness will kill any hope we have of ever being free, forgiven, and able to live in some kind of reasonable peace with ourselves.

Don't get me wrong, though, there is a lot to be said for self-righteousness.

In the last chapter, I told you about my impossible job. I'm a preacher, and in this day and age, that is not one of the most desired jobs in our culture. Even the word *preacher* has some very negative connotations attached to it (e.g. "preachy"). In fact, you may wonder why in the world a reasonably sane and intelligent guy would choose this profession.

It wasn't always this way. I can remember when the local preacher was respected. Even the newspapers took his or her comments seriously, quoting them as authority. Not only that. I can remember when department stores gave clergy discounts to preachers and country clubs gave them complimentary memberships.

Those days are long gone.

If you want to stifle conversation at a party, when someone asks you what you do, tell him or her that you're in vinyl repair, or you're a preacher. In both cases, people will yawn, say "really?," and then avoid you for the rest of the evening.

Okay. Why do I do it? It's a God thing, and I can't help it.

To be honest, there are other reasons as well. At the seminary where I teach, one of the funny comments going around is this: "They give the preacher a microphone, shine a spotlight on him, put his image on a very large screen, place him six feet above everybody else . . . and then they tell that preacher to be humble."

Good point.

Being a preacher allows me to feel self-righteous (and as I mentioned, there is a lot to be said for self-righteousness). It allows me to say what I think, even if it's stupid, without being stoned (it's been a lot of years since a preacher was stoned in America). Better yet, if you manage to write books or do media, people interview you and some even think you are a god or a reasonable facsimile of same.

That is not bad until the pain gets greater than the payback. If you aren't very righteous (even if everybody thinks you are), if you say things that aren't existentially true (even if people think they are), and if you start wincing at the phoniness (even if you hide it well), you experience great pain. And if you don't do something about it, it will kill you emotionally, spiritually, and even physically.

I recently preached at a church I had attended when I was much younger. The video people (they thought it was funny) put a photo of me on the big screen that was taken thirty years before. When I got up to speak, people started laughing. I looked up at the photo and said, "Go ahead and laugh." Then pointing to myself I said, "This is what the church did to me . . . and I wouldn't have done it for anyone else but Jesus."

That was a lie! The church didn't do anything to me. I did it to myself.

Maybe you have too.

Preachers aren't the only ones into self-righteousness. Most Christians (and pagans, conservatives, liberals, progressives, everyone else) are too. You see it in the "gotcha" politics of our culture, in the halls of academia where position and publishing are everything, inside abortion clinics where abortions are performed by "pro-choice" advocates, and outside the same clinics where "pro-life" advocates picket and pray. It comes from talking heads on television and hosts of talk shows paid big bucks to pontificate. It is on the editorial pages of every newspaper in the world. Self-righteousness is the stuff of Tea Parties on the right and fund-raisers on the left. It is like a weed that is everywhere and nearly impossible to get rid of.

Recently a well-known and popular author denounced her Christianity on her Facebook page. While she made it clear that she was not walking away from Jesus, she was tired of Christians and Christianity. Then she made a list of what irritated her about us. She said that if being a Christian meant being antigay, antifeminist, and antiprogressive, she was here and now declaring herself no longer a Christian.

The day she wrote that, I was a guest on a radio talk show. Among other questions, I was asked what I thought about this woman's words. I said that it was rare to encounter that much self-righteousness and arrogant drivel coming from one person. "Maybe," I said, "she will grow up someday and blush. It's incredibly sophomoric and reminds me of a first-year music student criticizing Bach."

And you know something? It felt so good to say it! It's hard to critique self-righteousness without being self-righteous.

Self-righteousness is addictive and, as with most addictions, more and more of the drug is required to get that initial kick. When it starts, it feels good, but before long we're waiting for a vacancy in the Trinity and wondering where all our friends have gone. Self-righteous folks only hang out with other self-righteous folks, and that's the stuff of which revolutions and churches are made. There is, of course, a difference between self-righteousness and convictions. I have some strong and conservative political and theological convictions. I believe those convictions are true and other "truths" that contradict those convictions are false. That almost goes without saying. However, it is a short trip between convictions and self-righteousness. And the real problem is that one hardly ever remembers making the trip.

The most salient thing about self-righteousness is that it creates blindness. In other words, self-righteousness is hardly ever diagnosed or ac-

> *It is a short trip between convictions and self-righteousness.*

knowledged by someone who is self-righteous. This disease is killing us, and the tragedy is that we don't even know it.

The late Henri Nouwen moved from a career of fame, fortune, and academic acceptability to taking care of handicapped adults. At his death, that was his calling. Nouwen said that the change forced him to rediscover his true identity. What he wrote about that experience is profound: "These broken, wounded, and completely unpretentious people forced me to let go of my relevant self—the self that can do things, show things, prove things, build things—and forced me to reclaim that unadorned self in which I am completely vulnerable, open to receive and give love regardless of any accomplishments. I am telling you all this because I am deeply convinced that the Christian leader of the future is called to be completely irrelevant and to stand in this world with nothing to offer but his or her own vulnerable self. That is the way Jesus came to reveal God's love."[4]

Mark Twain once said to a group of self-sufficient people that they would one day meet someone who was happy and had nothing. When it happened, they would find out that they had "paid too much for their whistle." That is the way I feel when I read that quote.

How about you? Did you pay too much for your whistle? How's it working for you so far?

Maybe a few free sins are exactly what the doctor ordered.

The sacrifices of God are a broken spirit;

a broken and contrite heart, O God, you will not despise.

—Psalm 51:17

Those who are well have no need of a physician,

but those who are sick. . . .

I came not to call the righteous, but sinners.

—Matthew 9:12–13

3

. . .

Repent! The End Is Near!

You may not know it, but unbelievably rich spiritual power is available to you. This spiritual power is not the result of being more religious, acquiring more knowledge about God, moving to a monastery, being more obedient, or praying more often. I suppose there is nothing wrong with those things, but they don't yield spiritual power.

The source of spiritual power is repentance.

Wait, wait. Before you burn this book, repentance isn't what you think it is. It's so very different from what most people think that I tried to find another word for it. When the word *repentance* comes up, most of us think of a weird little man holding a sign that reads, "Repent! The end is near!" or some kind of other "turn or burn" message directed at horrible sinners to scare the hell out of them.

That's not what repentance is at all. In fact, it's a wonderful word. I have some good news for you.

REPENTANCE IS . . .

Repentance is from a Greek word meaning "to change one's mind." When it is applied in a biblical sense, it doesn't mean changing your ways (or else!). It means that you recognize God is God and you aren't. It means that you don't get a vote on what is right and what is wrong. It means that when you recognize God's authority, you go to God and tell him so. In short, repentance is knowing who you are, who God is, what you've done or haven't done, and then going to God in agreement with him and his assessment.

That's it?

Yes, that's it.

Repentance isn't changing; it's God's way of changing us if that is what he wants. Changing, though, isn't even the issue. If the Bible is right in that all our sins are covered by the sacrifice of Christ on the cross and Christ gives us his righteousness in place of our sinfulness, change may happen, but it isn't what this whole thing is about. (More on that later.)

Listen to the words of the Heidelberg Catechism in answer to the question, "How are you right with God?"

Only by true faith in Jesus Christ. Even though my conscience accuses me of having grievously sinned against all God's commandments and of never having kept any of them, and even though I am still inclined toward all evil, nevertheless, without my deserving it at all, out of sheer grace, God grants and credits to me the perfect satisfaction, righteousness, and holiness of Christ, as if I had never sinned nor been a sinner, as if I had been as perfectly obedient as Christ was obedient for me. All I need to do is to accept this gift of God with a believing heart.[1]

But I'm getting way ahead of myself.

Let me tell you something that might shock you. Your disobedience, your failure, your rebellion, your struggle to be better—in short, your sin—is the greatest gift God has given you *if you know it*. Not only that. Your obedience, your faithfulness, your success, and your getting better is the most dangerous place you can be *when you know it*.

The anger of Jesus was never directed at those who were great sinners, but at those who seemed not to be. In fact, he said, "Unless your righteousness exceeds that of the scribes and Pharisees [the most patently righteous people Christ's hearers knew], you will never enter the kingdom of heaven" (Matthew 5:20). And just a cursory reading of Matthew 23 should make the most religious, obedient, and righteous among us wince. There Jesus pronounces seven woes on religious people. It's not pretty.

Free sins are a gift—but only if you know you need them. Repentance is a source of great power, but only if you know you need to repent.

BURNING BRIDGES

A number of years ago on our broadcast I answered a question about homosexuality. I was clear about homosexual sin being no different than any other sin and that Christ loved and died for all kinds of sinners. I probably said what I often say (something I got from our producer) about the issue: that one often hears fat preachers yelling at gay guys, but rarely do you hear gay guys yelling at fat preachers. I made it clear that none of us could throw rocks at anybody from our position of purity. "But," I said, "with that being said, I simply can't call right what God calls wrong or say that something isn't sin that God calls sin. I can't erase what the Bible says about anything. When I try to do that, it always leaves a smudge on the page. God has this thing about celibacy outside of marriage, and he directs his comments to everybody, gay or straight."

You should have read the letter I got from a prominent and well-known leader of the gay community. He was ticked! It was one of those "Who do you think you are?" kinds of letters. Contrary to my usual response to those kinds of letters (i.e., "You may be right . . . but you're probably wrong"), I took his letter seriously and wrote to him the following:

> *I really didn't mean to offend you. It would be crazy for someone who is as big a sinner as I am to throw rocks at you, and I didn't mean to do that. My problem isn't your sin or my sin.*

My problem is that when either of us contradicts God, we burn the bridge that he has provided for us to get to him and get loved . . . loved far beyond anything you can imagine. The issue isn't whether you or I change, become obedient, or "shine for Jesus." The issue is that bridge. The difference is that I cross over that bridge and get hugged and you've burned it . . . and you burned it because you don't think you need it.

The second letter I received from my new friend was far gentler than the first. He said that he had always been a bit uncomfortable with his lifestyle and that, if something happened to his

> *When either of us contradicts God, we burn the bridge that he has provided for us to get to him and get loved.*

relationship with his significant other, he didn't think he would establish another relationship like that. It's a long story and involves a lot of letters, a lot of honesty, and a lot of pain. The point I'm making here is that my friend didn't become perfect, but he did learn to "run to Jesus." He now knows how very much he is loved, accepted, and forgiven.

Burning the bridge wasn't just my friend's problem; it's my problem too. And therein is what I perceive to be the greatest problem most (maybe all) people—especially Christians—have with God and other people. I've already brought up the subject, but let's talk about it again. The problem is self-righteousness. Self-righteousness is killing us, robbing us of power, and making the good news God gave to the world into something very, very different from what God intended.

Philipp Melanchthon, Martin Luther's colleague in the Reformation, was a pharisee of sorts. Luther needed Melanchthon, but he wasn't altogether happy with his arrogance and perfectionism. Luther told Melanchthon that he ought to just go out and sin so he would have something to repent of.

When Luther told his followers to "sin boldly!" he wasn't encouraging sin. He was encouraging repentance and a bold new trust in the sufficiency of Christ for all sin. Luther once suggested to a man who questioned him about encouraging sin that there was an incredible arrogance in assuming that anything we could ever do would be more sufficient than the blood of God's own Son.

That's why I say, *you get three free sins!*

Not just that—you get unlimited free sins!

So go and "sin boldly."

Steve, I'm shocked! How could you?

I don't know why you're shocked. When you joined the church (if you're a Christian), you announced to the world that you were sinful and seriously screwed up. The church, someone has said, is the only club in the world where the only qualification for joining it and staying in it is that one be unqualified. The Bible and systematic theology tell us that we are sinners who sin. The church's confessions of faith add that same assessment. The liturgies have prayers of confession. All point to the fact that we're screwed up . . . and not just a little bit.

THE POWER OF REPENTANCE

The *Book of Common Prayer* (as well as liturgical books throughout the church) has these words of general confession: "Almighty God, Father of our Lord Jesus Christ, maker of all things, judge of all men: We acknowledge and bewail our manifold sins and wickedness, which we from time to time most grievously have committed, by thought, word, and deed, against thy divine Majesty, provoking most justly thy wrath and indignation against us."[2]

That's not a prayer we pray only before joining the church. It is the ongoing heart (or ought to be) of every believer and every church. It is repentance, the source of our power and authenticity. It is the walk to which we have been called. As Christians, we have not been called to tell the world how good we are and how God made us that way. We have been called to stand before God and the world, as it were, naked, honest, and loved. In this state—and this state alone—we find power at its purest and best.

Now if you aren't into this Christian thing, you're probably cheering me on. *Yeah,* you're thinking, *it's time someone finally said what needs to be said to those hypocrites! You go, bro!*

But not everyone recognizes the value of repentance and the power it brings. Do you remember when Brit Hume—former ABC chief White House correspondent and now FOX senior political analyst—talked about Tiger Woods after his worst sins and foibles had become public? Hume (a Christian who doesn't talk about it often but doesn't try to hide it either) said that Tiger Woods needed redemption and forgiveness. Hume suggested that Buddhism (Woods's religious preference) didn't deal with those issues (which, by the way, is true and not a negative comment about Buddhism, as any Buddhist will tell you), and redemption and forgiveness were exactly what Woods needed. Hume went on to say that forgiveness and redemption are exactly what is offered by Jesus Christ. (Given the way Tiger Woods has been playing of late, he certainly could use something. Who knows? It could be that forgiveness might help his game.)

Be that as it may, what Hume said would have caused far less controversy if Hume had announced that he had joined al-Qaeda and decided to work to destroy America. Judging by the almost universal reaction of most major media outlets and pundits to Hume's words, you would have thought that Brit Hume was an arrogant, shallow hypocrite. In fact, he was just the opposite. Hume made it clear that everybody is in great need of redemption and forgiveness.

The truth is that Hume wasn't the hypocrite; everybody else was. The self-righteous drivel aimed at Hume would have made the most arrogant Pharisee blush. I know because I'm quite good at hypocrisy and self-righteousness myself. Just as it takes a farmer to really identify BS, it takes a preacher to recognize self-righteousness . . . a preacher who has been there, done that, and who is still pretty good at it.

Just so you know, the need for repentance, redemption, and forgiveness is universal. I don't care if you are a liberal or a conservative, a religious fanatic or a militant atheist, a "spiritual"/"religious" person or someone who runs from all of that. It doesn't matter to me if you listen to Billy Graham or follow Camus—*you* are in need. No one in the human race is exempt.

It's in our DNA. I'm not your mother. But if you apply some of the principles I'm teaching in this book, you'll be better, happier, and far more effective than you are now. You'll also find that you have power you never knew you had.

When we finally acknowledge our need for forgiveness and come to God in repentance, we find true power: for we now have nothing to hide or protect, we don't care what people say or think about us, we are willing to speak truth gently, and we are enabled to speak it with tremendous, supernatural power.

THE PROBLEM WITH SELF-RIGHTEOUSNESS

The problem with self-righteousness (the opposite of repentance) is that not only is it in our DNA, and not only does it create blindness to its existence, but it is also addictive (as I mentioned in the last chapter). Self-righteousness is addictive because it makes us feel good, and after a while it defines who we are and how we see ourselves. It creates an "us and them" mentality and "us" is always right.

Let me show you the process:

> *Self-righteousness is addictive because it makes us feel good.*

self-righteousness starts with convictions (a good thing), then moves to discussion (another good thing), and finally falls into the devil's trinity of dismissal, demonization, and destruction (some very bad things).

John Frame, my colleague at Reformed Theological Seminary where I teach, is one of the finest theological minds of our time. He has said that refusal to talk (i.e., the spurious assumption that I'm right and you're wrong and that's all there is to it) is a sign of heresy. I think that refusal to talk is also a sign of self-righteousness. Why talk seriously to those cretins when they're obviously wrong (immoral, shallow, sinful, unthinking, hateful, ugly, uncompassionate, and lacking in convictions, education, and insight) and I'm obviously right (moral, profound, righteous, sensitive, and with credentials)? There is nothing more addictive than being in what C. S. Lewis called "the inner ring" while all of those horrible philistines are on the outside.[3]

I run in mostly conservative political and theological circles, and my convictions are conservative. Back when President Clinton was in office, I would often say to the audiences where I would speak that I was angry about and bothered by the president. Sometimes people would even applaud in response.

"No, no," I would say, "you don't understand. I'm not talking about Monica. The thing that really bothers me about the president is the way he has given so many Christians the opportunity to be self-righteous. We had a grand opportunity to say, 'It could have been me given the right opportunity and that much power. I'm like the president—seriously needy and sinful. Let me tell you about Someone who loves me anyway.' We blew an opportunity big time!"

During President Clinton's tenure in the White House, I heard about a group of Christians and Jews meeting in a political forum. They were, I was told, for the most part conservatives who discussed their displeasure with the direction of the country. One lady said that she was greatly troubled by the president's behavior in the White House and bemoaned that we no longer had "heroes." "What am I going to tell my children when they see what is going on?" she asked. "Madam," a rabbi said, "you tell them the same thing you tell them about David, Abraham, and Jacob . . . that people are bent and God still rules."

I like that.

Ronald Rolheiser, in his book, *The Holy Longing*, writes:

To be connected with the church is to be associated with scoundrels, warmongers, fakes, child-molesters, murderers, adulterers, and hypocrites of every description. It also, at the same time, identifies you with saints and the finest persons of heroic soul within every time, country, race, and gender. To be a member of the church is to carry the mantle of both the worst sin and the finest heroism of soul . . . because the church always looks exactly as it looked at the original crucifixion. God hung among thieves.[4]

The reading of Scripture should make the self-righteous blush. Because he likes us, God told us the truth about our "heroes." The Bible is a record of deceit, sexual immorality, hypocrisy, disobedience, sin, and God's grace. It attests to the way God honors his name despite—not because of—the deceit, sexual immorality, hypocrisy, disobedience, and sin.

If you have any biographical works in your library that don't tell you both the good and the bad of their subjects, burn those books! They are not helpful. They are built on lies and will give you aspirations of something that you simply can't be . . . a hero who doesn't have a dark side. Just so, if you have a preacher, pastor, Bible teacher, or professor who doesn't point out the dark side of the biblical "heroes," don't buy a used car from him or her and, more important, don't listen to him or her teach on anything of importance. They do you a disservice. In fact, not knowing the sinful exploits of our biblical heroes will make you into a self-righteousness addict.

I know you're thinking that all this is a downer. It really isn't. Just the opposite. It is incredibly freeing.

BINGO!

Let me ask you a question: aren't you tired of pretending to be something you're not?

In the last chapter, I asked how you were doing so far. Well? What if you just came out and said that you're not doing so well, that you're struggling with goodness, that you're having trouble with being all that people want and think you should be? What if you just came out and said, "I'm tired of pretending to be something I'm not. From now on, you'll have to deal with a sinner who sins, who is needy, and who, even if trying, isn't doing very well sometimes"?

One time I spoke for the national gathering of my denomination and said some rather controversial things. After my session, I was confronted by a serious young man in a three-piece suit and a concerned look on his face. "Dr. Brown," he said, "what you said today grieved my heart!"

"Grieved your heart?" I responded. "There is nothing big enough here to grieve your heart. We're one of the smallest denominations in America, and I'm a peon. Find something bigger to grieve your heart!"

"You don't want to hear," he said quietly and with a godly patience, "what a fellow pastor says?"

I thought about it for a moment and said, "No, not really, but if you want to say something and be honest about it, I'll listen . . . at least awhile."

"I think," he said, his voice rising for the first time (really spiritual people don't shout, but he was close), "that you are arrogant, rude, and prideful."

Do you know what I said? I said: "Bingo! You have read me well, but I'm better than I was. Your heart would have been even more grieved five years ago, and it would be even more grieved if you knew the whole truth about me now."

We ended up talking for over an hour, and he eventually loosened his tie. All things considered, it was a rather honest and good discussion, but that's not the point. The point is how I felt when I said, "Bingo!" Once I said that, I had an incredibly wonderful feeling of freedom and joy.

Generally, I would have defended myself. (I'm quite good at doing that.) I would have engaged him in a debate and "eaten his lunch." (I have a glib tongue and know how to use it.) I may have worked to belittle him and his judgmental spirit. (Any preacher can do that well.) I didn't. I just told him that he had read me well.

Do you know what I experienced with that one word, "Bingo!"? I felt free and powerful. In fact, it felt so good I've decided to do it more. I call it the "Bingo Retort."

You're wrong!

Bingo! I've been wrong at least 50 percent of the time.

You're selfish.

Bingo! My mother said the same thing, and my wife knows it too.

> *Do you know what I experienced with that one word, "Bingo!"? I felt free and powerful.*

You're not living up to your potential.

Bingo! If it's okay with you, I'm not going to live up to my potential awhile longer.

You're not fit to be a Christian.

Bingo! That's why Christ died for me.

You're a preacher? You're certainly not spiritually qualified to be a preacher.

Bingo! I've often said the same thing to God.

How can you be a Christian and say/do that?

Bingo! I sometimes wonder that myself.

I am follically challenged ("bald" for the slower among us). It didn't happen overnight. I didn't just look in the mirror one morning to discover that my hair was missing. It was incremental and slow.

I did what every bald guy tries to do at the beginning . . . hide the baldness. I moved hair around to those places where growth was sparse. But trying to hide baldness is sort of like self-righteousness. One doesn't even know it or admit it or think that anybody else notices it until a good wind destroys the ruse and everybody sees the truth. It starts with lowering the part of one's hair and eventually it comes to growing the hair long where it will grow and brushing it to cover the places where it won't. There were even times when I refused to take speaking engagements— I can't believe I'm telling you this!—because I wouldn't have time to "fix" my hair and cover my baldness.

It was my atheist friend who messed up the gig. "Can I ask you a question?" he said.

"Of course."

"You a preacher?"

"You know I am."

"How the h___ can you be a preacher who is into honesty and stuff like that and be that dishonest with your hair? Frankly, it's not only dishonest, it looks silly. Don't you know that everybody knows it and that they laugh behind your back?"

I don't remember what I said to him, but I do remember what I did that evening. I stood in the mirror and gave up. I cut off the long hairs I used to cover my bald head with and brushed what was left straight back. I was kind of surprised. I didn't look handsome exactly, but there was something to be said for joining the ranks of Yul Brynner, Patrick Stewart, Telly Savalas, and Michael Jordan. And I slept better that night, better than I had in a very long time. I was even able to sleep late because I didn't have to get up so early to "fix" my hair.

"Free at last! Thank God Almighty! Free at last!"

That experience was not dissimilar to the experience I had when I finally accepted the free sins God gave me.

Try it sometime! You'll be surprised by how you feel when you do. You see, self-righteousness isn't the only thing that's addictive. Repentance is too!

Be kind to one another, tenderhearted,

forgiving one another, as God in Christ forgave you.

—Ephesians 4:32

He was wounded for our transgressions;

he was crushed for our iniquities;

upon him was the chastisement that brought us peace

and with his stripes we are healed.

—Isaiah 53:5

4

· · ·

Why Can't We All Just Get Along?

If you let your dog do his business on your neighbor's lawn, cheat on your spouse or on tests, destroy reputations by spreading terrible rumors about your friends, hurt people with your anger, or make an obscene gesture at drivers who cut you off in traffic and you feel guilty about it, I'm here to help.

Go to www.thepublicapology.com.

That's a website (really) where you can apologize, ask for forgiveness, and, as they say, "feel less bad about your own misdeeds, past or recent" when you read other people's apologies. Confession, I suppose, is good for the soul; and if the Jesus thing doesn't work for you, that might.

My favorite apology on that website is this: "I apologize, Henry, for calling you a hypochondriac. You really were sick after all. Lorena."

Wonder what happened? It could be that Henry has cancer or he's in the hospital after surgery. It could be that Lorena caught whatever he had and is now suffering the way he was. Then again, perhaps the doctor told Henry he's terminal and that was reported back to Lorena. Maybe he died and they put on his gravestone, "I told you I was sick!"

Whatever it was, I do hope Lorena feels better.

But in this chapter, I'm not as much concerned with Lorena as I am with Henry. Henry has a great opportunity to be free and whole, but I doubt that "website repentance" from Lorena is going to do it for him. In fact, if Henry is reading this book (one never knows), I'm going to say some things that will change his life. In fact, what I'm going to teach him and you is a whole lot better than Lorena's confession. I'll begin by telling you two stories of forgiveness: one about the Journey of Forgiveness in Canada and another about a young man in Rwanda.

STORIES OF FORGIVENESS

My friend, Steve Boone, managing director of Northern Connections Christian Fellowship in Canada, told me about the Journey of Forgiveness and Kenny Blacksmith, former deputy grand chief of the Cree Nation of Quebec. Then on our talk show, *Steve Brown Etc.*, Steve introduced me to Barry Maracle—a First Nations pastor in Canada and a Mohawk. I listened to Barry tell a story that was almost unbelievable. In fact, I still shake my head in wonder when I think about it.

It started when the prime minister of Canada, Stephen Harper, a confessing Christian, extended a surprising apology on behalf of Canada, asking forgiveness of the First Nations, Inuit, and Métis people. Up to that point, there had been a number of political and social efforts (with varying degrees of success) at reconciliation, some including restitution to the native peoples of Canada. This was different.

In 1928 Canada tried to end its "Indian problem" by creating church-run, government-funded residential schools for native children in order to "prepare them" for life in white society. It meant the virtual kidnapping of thousands of Indian children with the intention of destroying their heritage. The stories of physical, sexual, and emotional abuse are many and disturbing. The last residential school was closed in 1996.

I don't have the time to cover the history of the inhumanity of Canada to its native peoples. It would only give you (and me) a grand opportunity to feel self-righteous. While what happened in Canada is tragic and horrible, it is not the exception; it's the rule. World history is replete with stories of the misuse of power and the destruction of those without power. Fact is, that story can be repeated over and over again in world history. No nation and no peoples have pure hands. It's everywhere and is at least one definition of world history.

So, in that sense, the horror of Canada shouldn't surprise you; it certainly doesn't surprise this cynical old preacher.

Let me tell what is surprising: in June of 2010, representatives and leaders from Canada's First Nations, Inuit, and Métis communities, the churches of ten providences and three territories, and international observers all gathered at the Ottawa Civic Center to formally and publicly extend forgiveness to the government of Canada and to experience and celebrate the freedom and joy that forgiveness imparts.[1]

That event didn't stop in Ottawa. In fact, the fire of forgiveness is catching all over the world and changing lives in incredible ways. There is a joy and a release in it that could change the world. That can only come with forgiveness.

I'm never surprised by sin—national sin, racial sin, political sin, your sin, or my sin. But forgiveness? That's different. When it happens, there is something supernatural and powerful afoot. Maybe that is why God has such a big thing about forgiveness.

One more story and then we'll get down to the real discussion.

Another story of forgiveness that has the same "smell of Jesus" comes out of Rwanda. Catherine Claire Larson's wonderful book, *As We Forgive*, chronicles the story of the Rwandan geno-

> I'm never surprised by sin. But forgiveness? That's different.

cide where 800,000 Rwandans were slaughtered in the span of one hundred days. You can, of course, read that history in many places. It's a story of baptized Christians with blood on their hands, of hatred created for political and economic power, and of incredible torture and killing rivaling that of the Third Reich.[2]

Ms. Larson begins her book with a reference to a seventeen-year-old boy by the name of Emmanuel whose horrible scars are a metaphor for Rwanda. They reflect, Ms. Larson says, the human capacity for evil and the amazing capacity of humans to heal from the unthinkable and to forgive. She writes:

> One of the names given to Jesus Christ was Emmanuel, or "God with us." Christ lived into his name. He was "with us" in that he took on human flesh and walked among us. He was "with us" in carrying both our sins and our sorrows to the cross. When God raised this man, Jesus Christ, from the dead, he didn't take away his scars. These scars testify to his pain, to his love, and to the extent to which God will go to conquer the evil of the world through the active suffering of forgiveness. Only through such active love can such scars of horror be transfigured into emblems of triumph. . . . Pain does not have to have the last word. Forgiveness can push out the borders of what we believe is possible. Reconciliation can offer us a glimpse of the transfigured world to come.[3]

Don't get caught up in the politics of the stories I just told you. Even though there is something to be said for "national repentance,"[4] I'm not writing a brief about it. In fact, I'm not even talking about repentance but about forgiveness. The reason I told you about the Journey of Forgiveness and Emmanuel is that these stories constitute a macrocosm (big stuff) of the microcosm (little stuff), which is you and me. These stories reflect the power God creates in personal lives when we see and practice God's call to forgive. And besides that, if these people can forgive what was done to them, you and I can forgive anything.

WHY CAN'T WE ALL JUST GET ALONG?

We can't get along because we find it impossible to let go (the meaning of the word *forgive*) of the injustice and pain others have caused us. *They* are the ones who need free sins; certainly not us. And not only that—it will be a cold day in a hot place before a holy, just, and righteous God forgives them. Let justice roll down like waters . . . and let it begin with the justice they deserve.

Really?

You will remember when Jesus' disciple Peter was frustrated. Evidently he had a friend who quite often needed to be forgiven. Peter wanted to have some boundaries and asked Jesus how often he had to forgive this man. Peter said he had already forgiven him seven times and that seemed sufficient. Jesus astounded Peter by saying, "I do not say to you seven times, but seventy times seven [i.e., forgiveness without limit]" (Matthew 18:22).

Then Jesus told Peter a story that is both instructive and radical. It's about a servant who owed his master a whole lot of money. Just before the servant was sent off to jail and his family was sold into slavery, the servant fell to his knees before his master and pleaded for mercy. The master forgave the debt.

Then in an astonishing display of disingenuous arrogance, the man—who had just been forgiven a major debt himself—refused to forgive a fellow servant a small debt; and he had him thrown in jail. When the master heard about it, he was ticked, called the unforgiving servant back, and said, "You wicked servant! I forgave you all that debt because you pleaded with me. And should not you have had mercy on your fellow servant, as I had mercy on you?" (18:32–33). Then the master threw his sorry posterior into jail.

Jesus said, "So also my heavenly Father will do to every one of you, if you do not forgive your brother from your heart" (v. 35).

Jesus was big on forgiveness. In the short prayer he taught his disciples, he included "forgive us our debts, as we also have forgiven our debtors" (Matthew 6:12). He said that before we offer a sacrifice in worship, we should leave it on the altar and do some heavy forgiving in order to restore any broken relationship (see Matthew 5:23–24). He made incredible promises about the power of prayer and then added a proviso by saying, "And whenever you stand praying, forgive, if you have anything against anyone" (Mark 11:25).

I could go on and on, but just a cursory reading of the Gospels shows that forgiveness wasn't just a casual sidebar to Christ's teaching. It was central and repeated often.

Why do you suppose Jesus emphasized forgiveness? Because he wanted us to be "nice"? Because he didn't care about justice? Because he was naive about human evil and what we do to one another? Because "gentle Jesus, meek and mild" simply didn't grasp the horror of injustice?

You've got to be kidding!

Forgiveness was the focal point in Christ's teaching because he knew that without profound "to the bone" forgiveness, there is no freedom, no real joy, no peace, and no release from the pain and the root of bitterness that destroys nations, families, and individuals. He understood that the key to everything important in life is forgiveness.

So he told us to do it!

The problem is that we can't on our own.

It's not that, in our finer moments, we don't want to. It isn't that we don't understand what he said. It isn't that we disagree with what he taught us. Sometimes it's just . . . well . . . impossible. "Forgive and forget" sounds good unless you're the one who feels the pain, and the more pain, the harder it is to forgive and forget.

What's the solution?

Three free sins!

I'm getting ahead of myself, so stay with me and I'll show you something that will change everything in your life. It's not

> *It isn't that we disagree with what he taught us. Sometimes it's just ... well ... impossible.*

easy (we'll address that in a later chapter), but it is "doable." Not only is it doable, it's a key to the door of joy and freedom that you simply can't get anywhere else.

IT ALWAYS STARTS WITH JESUS

It has to start with Jesus. If it doesn't, we don't have a prayer. In fact, without him, what he taught and, far more important, what he did, we can forget about forgiveness. Get a gun and settle scores!

There is an amazing prophecy in Isaiah 53 referring (Christians believe) to Jesus. The specifics are so detailed that when Isaiah 53 is read without a reference, almost everyone assumes it's from the New Testament and is quite surprised to find that it was written over seven hundred years before anybody had ever heard of Jesus.

One of the major themes in the book of Isaiah is the coming Messiah who will finally set things right. Everybody expected it would happen but didn't know when. And everybody expected the Messiah to be big and mean—bigger than the enemies of God's people who had oppressed them and mean enough to be their worst nightmare.

Then Isaiah referred to a "servant." That was unexpected and, even worse, confusing. Instead of explaining, Isaiah made it even more unexpected and confusing by describing the Messiah/Servant as one who suffers horribly and is killed. Isaiah 53 will take your breath away. Aside from being quite beautiful, Isaiah 53 points to something that is so profound and overwhelming that it is hard to absorb.

Messiah would not be very attractive ("no form or majesty that we should look at him, and no beauty that we should desire him"), he would not be popular ("he was despised and rejected by men"), and he would not be the "happy face" of religion ("a man of sorrows, and acquainted with grief") (vv. 2–3). That's bad enough, but then we read the statements (vv. 5–7, 10) that shake the very foundations of everything we believe, everything we thought and everything we expected:

> But he was wounded for our transgressions;
> he was crushed for our iniquities;
> upon him was the chastisement that brought us peace,
> and with his stripes we are healed.
> All we like sheep have gone astray;
> we have turned—every one—to his own way;
> and the LORD has laid on him
> the iniquity of us all.
> He was oppressed, and he was afflicted,
> yet he opened not his mouth;

like a lamb that is led to its slaughter,
      and like a sheep that before its shearers is silent,
      so he opened not his mouth.
. . . Yet it was the will of the LORD to crush him.

I've been talking about free sins, but you and I both know that forgiveness isn't cheap. Forgiveness always costs someone something. We have this spurious idea that forgiveness is simply a matter of saying, "I forgive you," and then going on about our lives. It doesn't work that way.

For instance, if I steal from you and you forgive me, it's going to cost you whatever I stole. If you strike me and I forgive you, it's going to cost me the pain of

> *I've been talking about free sins, but you and I both know that forgiveness isn't cheap.*

your blow. If I gossip about you and hurt your reputation, and you forgive me, it may cost you your reputation. If you have been abused and you forgive your abuser, it will cost you the emotional damage abuse brings.

Who is going to pay for the sins of the world? Bingo! How much is it going to cost? You and I have no idea! We can't come even close to putting our arms around it. We simply can't count that far, go that deep, or think that big. It's beyond us even as it moves us deeply. At least we do get that there is a profound sadness at the very heart of the cosmos. The sound of God's weeping as he "crushed" his own Son was heard throughout heaven.

But even in his agony, in all of his greatness and power, a holy God bends down low and witnesses our tears as they strike the ground. His tears mingle with ours in an astounding act of sacrifice on a cross planted on a garbage heap, between two thieves.

Have you ever been puzzled by the tears of Jesus in Luke 19:41–44 as he looked out over the city of Jerusalem? We understand the incident that happened just after the tears. Jesus went into the temple and kicked out the scoundrels. That's the God we know! "You go, Jesus!"

But what's with the tears?

Now you know.

I once spoke for a chapel service at a state prison. The chaplain printed up a bulletin for that service with a cover showing a prisoner in prison garb and a number on the back of his shirt. He is kneeling before the cross where Jesus hangs. The caption read: "My God! I did that???"

Yes, he did. And not only that—I did it too. And just so you know, you are also culpable. You may look quite spiritual, sitting there reading a religious book, but you don't fool me. I've been a preacher too long and have listened to too many confessions, so I know your secrets—the ones you won't tell to anyone because you know they would kick you out. I know me and I know you. So relax. Nobody is going to embarrass you, so let the confession do its work.

I got a call this morning, which was passed on to me after first going through two staff people. The man who called was quite upset because he had heard a broadcast where I told the story of having two lesbians as my guests on a television show I did a number of years ago.

The man asked me if I would allow those lesbians into my church. "Well," I replied, "I think the church is a good place for sinners. They took me in."

"Don't you care about the purity of the church?" he asked.

"Of course I do. I just haven't found one yet."

"Mine is."

"Great!" I said. "I assume, then, that you've kicked out all the fat people, the greedy people, the lustful men, and those cantankerous folks. And you're the only one left."

That's when the conversation turned bad and he hung up. After I got over my anger, I felt so very sad. I wasn't sad because he was self-righteous or a pharisee. I'm pretty good at that myself. I was sad because he can't know the supernatural power and joy of forgiving someone who needs it. (I'm going to tell you about that in the next chapter.)

Let me share with you a disturbing confession of sin based on the Ten Commandments. It's the confession of Martin Bucer (1491–1551), the Protestant reformer. And frankly, it just scratches the surface.

I poor sinner confess to thee, O Almighty, eternal, merciful God and Father, that I have sinned in manifold ways against thee and thy commandments.

I confess that I have not believed in thee, my one

God and Father, but have put my faith and trust more in creatures than in thee, my God and Creator, because I have feared them more than thee. And for their benefit and pleasure, I have done and left undone many things in disobedience to thee and thy commandments.

I confess that I have taken thy holy Name in vain, that I have often sworn falsely and lightly by the same, that I have not always professed it nor kept it holy as I ought; but even more, I have slandered it often and grossly with all my life, words and deeds.

I confess that I have not kept thy Sabbath holy, that I have not heard thy holy Word with earnestness nor lived according to the same; moreover that I have not yielded myself fully to thy divine hand, nor rejoiced in thy work done in me and in others, but have often grumbled against it stoutly and have been impatient.

I confess that I have not honored my father and mother, that I have been disobedient to all whom I justly owe obedience, such as father and mother, my superiors, and all who have tried to guide and teach me faithfully.

I confess that I have taken life; that I have offended my neighbor often and grossly by word and deed, caused him harm, grown angry over him, borne envy and hatred toward him, deprived him of his honor and the like.

I confess that I have been unchaste. I acknowledge

all my sins of the flesh and all the excess and extrava-
gance of my whole life in eating, drinking, clothing
and other things; my intemperance in seeing, hearing
and speaking, and in all my life; yea, even fornication,
adultery and such.

I confess that I have stolen. I acknowledge my
greed. I admit that in the use of my worldly goods I
have set myself against thee and thy holy laws. Greedily
and against charity have I grasped them. And scarcely,
if at all, have I given of them when the need of my
neighbor required it.

I confess that I have born false witness, that I have
been untrue and unfaithful toward my neighbor. I
have lied to him, I have told lies about him, and I have
failed to defend his honor and reputation as my own.

And finally I confess that I have coveted the pos-
sessions and spouses of others. I acknowledge in sum-
mary that my whole life is nothing else than sin and
transgression of thy holy commandments and an incli-
nation toward all evil.

Wherefore I beseech thee, O heavenly Father, that
thou wouldst graciously forgive me these and all my
sins. Keep and preserve me henceforth that I may walk
only in thy way and live according to thy will; and all
of this through Jesus Christ, thy dear Son, our Saviour.
Amen.[5]

That just about covers it.

MERCY HAS COME RUNNING TO *YOU*!

Now some good news. If you have run to Jesus, mercy has come running to you! You have, in light of what I've just taught you, unlimited free sins. I don't care where you've been or where you are, what you've done or what you're doing, what you're smoking or drinking, who you're sleeping with or demeaning, who you've offended or who you've hurt, or where the bodies are buried . . .

You're forgiven!

That's a good start, but there's a whole lot more to come. It's such good news that I want to tell you now, but I'm running out of chapter space.

Let me close with a story about former president Bill Clinton. (I can't believe I'm doing this, given I'm a Republican who is so conservative that I think Rush Limbaugh is a Communist! I'm also sure, as everybody knows, that when Jesus comes back, he will be both a Republican and a Presbyterian.)

Shortly after the impeachment trial, I was watching a news conference where reporters interviewed President Clinton. Most of what happened in that news conference was expected—expected questions, expected answers, and expected spin.

And then the president said something profound and wonderful, so much so that I thought I misunderstood. A reporter asked Clinton if he was going to forgive those who had conducted the impeachment trial and who had brought the charges.

There was a very long pause. "Those who need forgiveness," he said quietly, "must give it."

Three free sins is an amazing and glorious gift. It's not just because we all need forgiveness. It's because we all need to forgive and, in the very act of forgiving, there is laughter—a laughter that is as profound and as important as the tears that caused it.

He shall judge between the nations,

and shall decide disputes for many peoples;

and they shall beat their swords into plowshares,

and their spears into pruning hooks . . .

neither shall they learn war anymore.

—Isaiah 2:4

What causes quarrels and what causes fights among you?

Is it not this, that your passions are at war within you?

—James 4:1

5

· · ·

Ain't Gonna Study War No More!

I received this from a friend: "You have to work hard to offend Christians. By nature Christians are the most forgiving, understanding, and thoughtful group of people I've ever dealt with. They never assume the worst. They appreciate the importance of having different perspectives. They're slow to anger, quick to forgive, and almost never make rash judgments or act in anything less than a spirit of love . . . no, wait! I was thinking of Labrador retrievers!"[1]

That's funny because everybody who has been around Christians for very long knows that Christians aren't like Labrador retrievers. We're more like bulldogs. Frankly, I'm glad. There is nothing worse than a Christian acting like a Labrador retriever.

I'm going to deal with the whole subject of the "wuss factor" soon, but let me say here that there is no magic formula to take away our human proclivity toward insecurity, anger, and hurting others. We don't get along because we are sinful and selfish. In other words, we're human. We get better, but we don't get well until we get "home" (see 1 John 3:2).

The question is: how do we get better?

The problem is that getting better is so very boring. Self-righteousness has its rewards. There is something so satisfying about feeling better than "them," getting perceived justice and watching books get balanced. But forgiving, loving, and letting go of justified anger . . . where's the satisfaction in that?

Let me share an interesting passage from the Bible. In Hebrews 12:1 the writer admonished his readers to "run with endurance the race." Then in the next verse he said that we should keep our eyes on Jesus who "for the joy that was set before him endured the cross." Not only that, the writer said that Jesus did it "despising the shame" of his execution.

WHAT'S SO GREAT ABOUT FORGIVENESS?

I understand why Jesus went to the Cross. What is so hard to understand is the joy thing and how that joy could be so good that it caused him to not even care about the shame. It can't be understood unless we ourselves experience the release, the peace, and the joy of forgiving someone who doesn't deserve it. And if joy is really the payback for forgiveness, the fact that Jesus forgave and covered "the sins of the world" means that his joy must have been huge.

People who forgive are crazy. They're crazy like a fox.

Do you know why? Because the gift that comes from forgiveness is always joy and freedom.

Do you sometimes wonder where the joy went?

Do you feel lonely and afraid?

Have you found that you don't laugh very much anymore?

Do you wonder where the peace that was promised went?

Do you find yourself angry and frustrated more than you should be?

Do you have trouble sleeping?

Are you so very tired of trying to be good?

Do you feel like your religion has made you more uptight than you were before you discovered it?

Do you feel lonely because your friends have rejected your commitment?

Has your stand for God separated you from others?

Are you pretending to be Christian more than experiencing its reality?

If that's you, it may be indigestion; but I think not. Let me show you. Think of the person who irritates you the most, the one who has hurt you the deepest, the one who deserves forgiveness the least—and then forgive him or her. I can't

> *Are you so very tired of trying to be good?*

promise that you won't ever feel lonely, afraid, sad, anxious, angry, and frustrated again or that you won't ever need sleeping pills. What I can say is that you will be surprised by how much better you are when you do what Jesus said to do.

One more thing before we get to the question of how to forgive.

There is a text in the Bible that has caused tremendous theological and ecclesiastical debate, but its implication (once you set aside the debate) is incredible. Jesus addressed Peter and his tremendous insight into the nature of Christ. Then Jesus said about Peter (and by implication, the church and all Christians), "I will give you the keys of the kingdom of heaven, and whatever you bind on earth shall be bound in heaven, and whatever you loose on earth shall be loosed in heaven" (Matthew 16:19).

The "keys of the kingdom"! Now that's power. If you're a Christian, God has given you amazing power to bind and loose others. You have the power to bless or curse, to build or destroy, and to create joy or inflict pain. Later on we'll talk about the power of Christians in the world, but for now try and remember that forgiveness is a win/win deal. The forgiver gets the payback and so does the forgiven.

So now, how does one forgive the unforgivable?

I already told you: three free sins!

FOUR "ALMOST" IMPOSSIBILITIES

Let me explain with four biblical truths, or, if you will, four "almost" impossibilities.

1. It's almost impossible to accept something we don't need.

Forgiveness is at the very heart of the Christian faith. It's not about getting better, becoming more religious, or following the rules so God will love you. It's all about forgiveness, dummy! Everything else is secondary. If we don't keep the main thing the main thing, then everything else will turn sour on us.

My late and beloved friend, Rusty Anderson, was with his granddaughter one time when she did something she should not have done. "Honey," he said, "don't do that."

"I'm sorry, Granddaddy," she said.

Five minutes later she did the very same thing. "I told you before, don't do that," Rusty said to her.

"I'm sorry, Granddaddy," she said again.

Shortly after that she did the very same thing again. He turned angry. "I've told you twice already, don't do that!"

"I'm sorry, Granddaddy."

"Sorry," he said, raising his voice, "isn't enough!"

That's when Rusty told me that he heard God say, "Funny, it was enough for me."

I have some very good news for you: it really *is* enough! The real problem is when you think you have enough.

A number of years ago, I spoke at a missions conference for religious leaders. God—who obviously thought it was funny—put me at the dinner table with one of the most uptight and angry men I've ever met. (Well, that may be an overstatement given that I meet a lot of uptight and angry people in my line of work. But he was certainly in the running.) When the conversation turned to the doctrine of entire sanctification, I worked really hard to be civil. (Entire sanctification is the doctrine that says a Christian can reach a place in his or her life when there is no longer any known sin.)

But then the man claimed the experience of entire sanctification for himself.

I said something quite profound: "You've got to be kidding!"

"No," he replied, "I'm not kidding. Holiness is never a kidding matter. God has granted me the victorious life, and I give him all the glory."

"What do you do with your pride?" I asked. "Seems to me that if you've won the medal for being the most humble man in your club and you wear it, they should take it away. Isn't it kind of sinful to tell me that you're entirely sanctified? In fact, I kind of think that if someone were entirely sanctified, he wouldn't even know it."

I don't remember what he said, but I do remember that he was quite angry, and I didn't have to sit at the same table with him anymore because he avoided me the rest of the week. That made both of us happier.

I heard a couple of years later that he had left the ministry because of a moral failure.

Was the problem his moral failure? Not even close. Sin goes without saying. His problem was that he couldn't forgive (certainly not me). This man couldn't forgive because he couldn't be forgiven . . . he thought he didn't need it. Jesus said people like that are like "whitewashed tombs, which outwardly appear beautiful, but within are full of dead people's bones and all uncleanness" (Matthew 23:27).

We are serious sinners—profoundly needy, deeply selfish, and incredibly rebellious . . . you included! In other words, we (you included) are in desperate need of three free sins. In fact, we (you included) need a whole lot more than that.

If you rejected what I just wrote above, I'm so very sorry. You'll never know—that is until you screw it up so badly you can no longer fix it or hide it—the laughter and freedom of being forgiven and the concomitant laughter and freedom of forgiving someone who is just as messed up as you are.

2. It's almost impossible to give something we don't have.

Do you know why recovering drunks hang out with and are comfortable around other recovering drunks? It is because they know forgiveness and how wonderful it is to forgive. The principle is this: you can't forgive until you've been forgiven, and then you can only forgive to the degree to which you've been forgiven. If you have received three free sins (i.e., unlimited free sins), you have a bank full of them, and other sinners will flock to you and your bank to draw on the account.

A friend once told me a story about a little boy, Billy. He was in the classroom working on his studies, and then to his horror, he looked down and saw a spreading puddle at his feet. When he realized what had happened, Billy was horrified and humiliated. The worst part was that the teacher was headed down the aisle his way. Billy didn't know what to do. There was no way to hide it or cover it. There was no way he could change it. He died inside as the teacher got closer and closer to his desk. Billy knew that the other children would make fun of him and he would never live it down.

Just as the teacher reached Billy's desk, his classmate Sally walked by carrying a fish bowl. She was going to change the water. When she got to Billy's desk, she slipped, spilling water all over him and all over the floor. Everybody, including the teacher, was quick to help clean up the mess. They thought it was one mess, but Billy knew it was two. He had been saved.

Later that day at the bus stop, Billy saw Sally and quietly said to her, "You did that on purpose, didn't you? That wasn't an accident, was it?"

"No," she said, "it wasn't an accident."

"Why did you do that?"

She smiled and said, "It happened to me once."

If you had been there that day, you would have noticed a little girl and a little boy holding hands and laughing. And you would have felt good even though you wouldn't have known "the rest of the story."

One time a prostitute crashed a dinner party for religious people. Jesus made an astounding statement. He forgave her sins and then said, "Therefore I tell you, her sins, which are many, are forgiven—for she loved much. But he who is forgiven little, loves little" (Luke 7:47).

3. It's almost impossible to fix something by ignoring what needs to be fixed.

I sometimes think that religion is mankind's effort to ignore the pain.

I was once asked to be the stand-in speaker at a conference for seniors who had served a very large ministry for much of their lives. They were financial contributors, volunteers, and ambassadors for that particular ministry. These were hard-core Christians who were leaders in their local churches and communities. And there were a number of pastors present too.

Because I was a last-minute substitute, hardly anybody knew who I was except in the vague sense that I was some speaker who had written books, did media, was fairly controversial, and was old like them.

I had been assigned four teaching sessions, and in that first session I gave them "three free sins." I knew it was probably not the smartest way to begin, especially when speaking to people who were faithful servants of Christ. But they didn't sleep during my talks after that, and they certainly weren't bored. Angry, upset, shocked—but not bored. (As I teach my seminary students, it really is much better to shock people than to bore them.)

I told them they had a reputation for godliness and everybody looked up to them as fathers and mothers in the faith. "But," I said, "I know the truth. I've been around a long time, and frankly, you and I both know that you aren't nearly as good as your reputation suggests. You have secrets that would shock everybody who knows you if they knew the truth. You're also scared spitless somebody will find out. If you promise not to tar and feather me until I'm finished, I'll help you. But if you leave before then, you'll miss something really good."

That's kind of what Jesus did.

Do you remember in Luke 5:17–26 when the friends of a paralytic brought him to Jesus for healing? These were good friends who loved their disabled friend and were willing to do anything to see him run and dance again. The problem was that the crowd was so big in the house where Jesus was teaching that they couldn't get near enough for Jesus to even notice they were there. So they got some tools, carried their friend up to the roof, tore a big hole in the ceiling, and lowered their friend down right in front of Jesus.

Now those were godly and committed friends. I don't know this, but I suspect that the paralytic was godly too.

How many people who are not believers and reasonably obedient and faithful would go to that much trouble to get to a faith healer?

Do you know what Jesus did? Instead of healing the paralytic, Jesus said, "Man, your sins are forgiven you" (v. 20).

I can imagine the disappointment of the paralytic and his friends. But that was nothing compared to the reaction of the religious leaders. They didn't care about the cripple or about the model of friendship from those who brought him. They didn't care about the faith—they were interested in theology.

Luke wrote, "And the scribes and the Pharisees began to question, saying, 'Who is this who speaks blasphemies? Who can forgive sins but God alone?'" (v. 21). Then Jesus said, "Why do you question in your hearts? Which is easier, to say, 'Your sins are forgiven you,' or to say, 'Rise and walk'? But that you may know that the Son of Man has authority on earth to forgive sins,"—he said to the man who was paralyzed—'I say to you, rise, pick up your bed and go home'" (vv. 22–24).

> *They didn't care about the cripple or about the friendship. They didn't care about the faith—they were interested in theology.*

What was going on? Everybody thought the man needed a physician, a magician, or a theologian—but what he really needed was to be forgiven!

So at the conference where nobody knew my name, I

decided that I would follow the pattern of Jesus, and so, in his name, I gave them free sins. They expected doctrinal purity (and I am doctrinally pure), a Bible teacher who would reaffirm the reality they had proclaimed in their service for Christ (and I did do that), and a reconfirmation of what they had believed all their lives and to which they had been faithful—far more faithful than most (and I granted them that). But first, and far more important than anything else, in the name of Christ, I gave them free sins.

I don't know when I've seen people more upset and angry. I was reasonably certain they weren't going to stone me (they were, after all, servants of Christ and gentlemen and women). But frankly, I think they weren't even sure I was saved. They thought I was, at best, a heretic who had lost his mind.

Then they started listening. I spent my sessions teaching what I've written in this book. Do you know what happened? Everything changed. I started out as the devil incarnate and ended up being an angel unawares. In fact, if it had been a football game, they would have dumped a keg of Gatorade over my head! I don't think I've ever been hugged that much. As my wife and I drove away from the conference, I told her, "That was the most affirming bunch of people I've ever seen."

Why do you suppose they were so affirming? Someone had told them what they needed to hear and not what they wanted to hear. Someone had told them what nobody else would—that despite their reputations and their service, they were needy and sinful, that I knew it and Jesus knew it and both of us liked them anyway. It was a joyous time, and it happened because, in the name of Jesus, I gave them permission to be human and forgiven.

As you know, I spend a considerable portion of my time talking with and teaching pastors and students preparing to be pastors. Those folks have an incredibly high degree of commitment. I've found that the greatest need among Christian leaders isn't for more commitment, more religion, and more "making an impact" for Jesus. What they need is to be taught that they are seriously sinful and God loves them anyway.

One more truth and perhaps the most important:

4. It's almost impossible to serve a King and ignore his passion and substitute your own.

Let me give you a scary text that keeps Christians up at night. Jesus said, "Not everyone who says to me, 'Lord, Lord,' will enter the kingdom of heaven, but the one who does the will of my Father who is in heaven. On that day many will say to me, 'Lord, Lord, did we not prophesy in your name, and cast out demons in your name, and do many mighty works in your name?' And then will I declare to them, 'I never knew you; depart from me, you workers of lawlessness'" (Matthew 7:21–23).

If you've been bludgeoned by that text, I have some astonishing news for you: Jesus was not talking about getting better, working harder, and being more religious so that, when the end came, he would recognize you. He was talking about what he had set loose in the world—the love and forgiveness that he had made possible. Jesus was talking to the most faithful and most religious people in his culture, and he called them false prophets. Immediately prior to that text, Jesus said that we would know the false prophets by their "fruit." And then Jesus said, "So, every healthy tree bears good fruit, but the diseased tree bears bad fruit. A healthy tree cannot bear bad fruit, nor can a diseased tree bear good fruit" (vv. 17–18).

Jesus said that he was a great physician who came for sick people. Even his name bore the meaning of his message. When Joseph, the supposed father of Jesus, was told about the birth of Jesus, an angel from God said this: "Joseph, son of David, do not fear to take Mary as your wife, for that which is conceived in her is from the Holy Spirit. She will bear a son, and you will call his name Jesus, *for he will save his people from their sins*" (Matthew 1:20–21, emphasis mine).

That's it? Yeah, that's it.

Jesus set loose power in the world by forgiving a whole lot of people a whole lot of sin when they didn't deserve it and never would. He said that "sorry was enough." And now those very people have the power to do the same thing for others who don't deserve it. The essence of the Christian faith is forgiveness—unbelievable forgiveness given by screwed-up people to other screwed-up people without any "kicker."

My friend Lea Clower is one of the bloggers on www.poopedpastors.com, our website for pastors. In one of his blogs, he tells the story of an elderly Chinese lady who carried water in two large pots,

> *The essence of the Christian faith is forgiveness—unbelievable forgiveness given by screwed-up people to other screwed-up people without any "kicker."*

each hanging on the ends of a pole she carried across her neck. One of the pots was perfect and one was cracked. For two years every day she carried water from the stream to her home and each time she did it, she arrived home with the perfect pot full of water and the cracked pot barely half full.

The perfect pot was proud of its accomplishments, but the poor, cracked pot was miserable and guilty and felt like a failure. One day the cracked pot spoke to the woman and told her how sorry it was: "I'm ashamed of myself because this crack in my side causes water to leak out all the way back to your house."

"Did you notice," the woman smiled and said, "that there are beautiful and healthy flowers on your side of the path?"

Forgiveness creates flowers. But like that pot, the flowers only grow, as we'll see, because of the crack.

I have a friend who was a missionary in a very hard place. She had served there for a number of years, and I felt that it was time for her to come home and rest. She had done her part. I asked her what she was going to do when she finished her sabbatical.

"I'm going back."

"You don't have to do that," I told her. "Jesus is pleased with what you've done. Why do you feel you have to go back?"

"Because," she said, "somebody has to plant flowers in hell."

When they saw the boldness of Peter and John,

and perceived that they were uneducated, common men,

they were astonished.

And they recognized that they had been with Jesus.

—Acts 4:13

Also [pray] for me, that words may be given to me in

opening my mouth boldly to proclaim the mystery of the gospel,

for which I am an ambassador in chains,

that I may declare it boldly, as I ought to speak.

—Ephesians 6:19–20

6

. . .

The Wuss Factor

I just finished reading Eric Metaxas's wonderful biography of Dietrich Bonhoeffer (*Bonhoeffer: Pastor, Martyr, Prophet, Spy*). Frankly, I've always been overwhelmed by the story of Bonhoeffer's courage. I didn't know where Bonhoeffer got it. In fact, there is no explanation for him. Bonhoeffer should have been simply a gentleman, enjoying his wealth, his piano, and his books. He was bright, of course, and had an incredible heritage; but he didn't have dirt under his fingernails. One expects courageous warriors to come from the ranks of the "common man," not from the privileged classes.

When I was a student at Boston University School of Theology, Bonhoeffer was (wrongly) identified as one of the fathers of the "God Is Dead" movement. He was seen as another example of a man whose liberal theology informed his concern for justice. Out of that concern, he became a martyr for the cause of the oppressed.

While I respect my colleagues and friends who hold to a theological position different from my orthodox views, I could never see how a position that was more humanistic than theological could inspire anybody to do anything—much less give his or her life for any cause.

THE COURAGE OF BONHOEFFER

But as I read Metaxas's book, I saw for the first time Bonhoeffer's profound relationship with Christ and understood that he was a major danger to the Third Reich and a "troubling thorn" in the liberal theological ranks of the German church—not despite his faith, but because of it. Bonhoeffer was dangerous because he was free, and he was free because he was forgiven.

Bonhoeffer wrote: "It is high time we broke with our theologically based restraint towards the state's actions—which, after all, is only fear. 'Speak out for those who cannot speak.' Who in the church today realizes that this is the very least that the Bible requires of us?"[1]

I once heard an Anglican bishop say to a group of frightened Christians, "If you Christians can get over your fear, you're going to be dangerous."

He was right, but the question is: how do we get over our fear?

Three free sins! That's how.

But I'm getting ahead of myself again.

FREEDOM CREATES DANGEROUS PEOPLE

A number of years ago I interviewed Jim Bakker—the disgraced television evangelist who went to prison—about his book *I Was Wrong: The Untold Story of the Shocking Journey from PTL Power to Prison and Beyond.*

I told Jim Bakker about an experience I had while speaking to a convention of religious broadcasters during the time of his arrest. Every one of those broadcasters (me included) suffered significant financial loss because of Bakker's actions. Not only that—he created a public relations disaster for all of us. We had every reason to be angry.

Just before I got up to speak, the organization's president stopped me and said, "Steve, I was just watching television and I saw them taking Jim Bakker off to prison. He was weeping. We need to pray for him."

I agreed and figured I would call on someone to pray for Bakker. I thought that I could find at least one "nice" Christian in the bunch who wouldn't pray that he got the hives. "Bill told me that he had just seen the police take Jim Bakker off to jail," I said. "He was crying and we probably need to pray for him."

Just when I got ready to ask someone to pray, to my astonishment, the entire group of people at the convention got up and quietly knelt down by their chairs and started praying for Bakker—for God to uphold him, to bless him, to forgive him, and to enable him to get through the pain, doubt, and confusion that he was, at that moment, experiencing.

After I told Jim Bakker that story, he was quite emotionally moved. I asked how he felt, and he said, "I feel loved, forgiven, and free."

Jim Bakker went on to describe the difference between having a successful national television ministry with millions of followers and finally getting out of prison and having nothing. I don't remember everything Bakker said in that interview. I do remember his humility and the quiet way he described his pain and his surprise at being released from prison early. I remember his description of the time Billy Graham visited him in prison and loved him, and about Jerry Falwell's visit and how hard it was to forgive Falwell for what Bakker perceived as Falwell's betrayal.

Although I don't remember the details, I'll never forget what Jim Bakker said about being loved and being free. He had done some really bad things, and yet he felt loved. Everybody knew what he had done and suspected that he could do it again, and yet he was free. He said, "I can go wherever I want—to a bar, a church, or a Wicca gathering—talk to anybody about anything, and nobody is shocked or surprised. I'm free for the first time in my life."

Prison, public humiliation, shame, and failure are a big price to pay for freedom. But then again, maybe not. In fact, it may have been worth it all. Jim Bakker is dangerous now, because he doesn't have anything to protect.

If you have enough free sins, you don't either.

Boldness is a very hard trait for Christians to acquire. In fact, in some cir-

> *Jim Bakker is dangerous now, because he doesn't have anything to protect.*

cles, boldness is considered a sin or, at best, in bad taste. If you must say what you think (and that should be rare), at least be nice about it and don't offend anyone.

Because of the default Christian position of niceness, Christians have to be careful when defining words like *forgiveness, love,* and *compassion* lest these words become yet other ways to be nice. Forgiveness always costs, love is sometimes as hard as nails, and compassion can degenerate into another form of do-goodism if one isn't careful.

Do you know the old story about the young woman driving a small, red sports car? She zipped in front of an elderly lady driving a big Mercedes and took the parking spot for which the Mercedes driver had been waiting. The elderly lady was really ticked but the young woman smiled and said, "That's what happens when you're young and quick."

Then to the surprise of the young woman, the elderly lady backed up and aimed her Mercedes right at the sports car and crashed into it. And then to the additional horror of the young woman, the elderly lady backed up and did it again. The young woman was livid. The elderly lady rolled down her window and said with a smile, "That's what happens when you're old and rich."

If you're old and rich, you can be dangerous. You don't have anything to protect.

You are, as it were, "old and rich" if you have free sins. It means that you're loved, covered, free, and dangerous.

I recently received an email from a dear pastor friend going through some hard times who felt ashamed, embarrassed, and guilty. Let me quote from that email:

Next to Jesus, my wife has been and is the best and most incredible friend and partner. She has been the instrument with flesh whom the Lord has used most in my sanctification process. I'm just blown away that she's still with me after almost 50 years of marriage.

One evening a couple of weeks ago, we were seated on a sofa in my study. We had been talking for some time about my feelings of shame, embarrassment, and humiliation when she told me that she loved me more than ever. I was absolutely blown away by that. I thought she might have feelings of regret for having hitched her wagon to mine or of anger for having to go through this experience with me. Instead, the Lord used her, once again, to show me how one person can show grace and unconditional love to another. I know for certain that when Solomon wrote, "Many women have done excellently, but you surpass them all" (Proverbs 31:29), he had her in mind.

It is no small thing to be loved when you're unlovable, to be forgiven the unforgivable, and to be supported when you've done nothing to deserve it. That's the gospel. And that's why free sins are so important. It's the good news that while there are those who might sacrifice for a *good* man or woman, "at the right time Christ died for the ungodly [that would be us!]. . . . God shows his love for us in that while we were still sinners, Christ died for us" (Romans 5:6, 8).

Religion can make you weird. It can also make you afraid. If God is a police officer at best and a child abuser at worst, you had better be careful, and *careful* will kill your freedom. If the work of Christ depends on your faithfulness, obedience, and purity, and you must work to maintain your witness, *maintaining* will kill your freedom. If there are angels piling up the good stuff you do on one side of some gigantic scale somewhere in heaven and demons piling up the bad stuff on the other side, you'll panic as the scale starts tipping in the wrong direction. That will make you quite meticulous about what you say, think, and do . . . and *meticulous* will kill your freedom.

I recently discovered the meaning of the story Jesus told about the talents (see Matthew 25:14–30).

> Religion can make you weird. It can also make you afraid.

I've taught the story a thousand times, so you'd think I would have gotten the meaning before now.

In this story, the master who was planning to go on an

extended trip had three servants to whom he entrusted some cash. He gave one servant five talents, another two, and the final servant one (talents were a certain amount of money). Then the master left. When he returned, the master called the servants before him to find out how they had handled what he had given them. The servant who received five talents used that money and made five more. The servant who received two talents doubled his as well. The master was pleased, gave each of them more, and said to both, "Well done, good and faithful servant."

Then with perspiration on his upper lip, the third servant approached the master. Knowing that the master was a hard man, the servant was afraid and had buried the money that had been given to him. "Here it is," he said, "all of it. You now have what is yours."

Jesus said that the master was ticked and kicked out the servant.

Fathers, mothers, preachers, and Christian teachers have used that story for two thousand years to scare the spit out of little boys and girls and everybody else with, "You're not living up to your potential. God has given you so much, and you had better use it or lose it. You don't want to be kicked out, do you? And don't you want to hear Jesus say, 'Well done, good and faithful servant'?"

Now I'm not against excellence and all, but that isn't even close to what Jesus was saying. If I hear one more preacher say in a funeral service (and I confess that before I learned the truth, I said it too) about the de-

ceased that God said, "Well done, good and faithful servant," I promise I'll set propriety aside and stand up and
yell, "That's nonsense! Only Jesus was faithful enough to
hear those words . . . certainly not Sam!"

So what was Jesus teaching?

In the next chapter in Matthew, as a result of what
Jesus just said, Matthew says that the chief priest and
the elders (i.e., the religious leaders) got together and
planned how they were going to kill Jesus. I would suggest
that one doesn't kill someone for teaching that little boys
and girls should work harder. It must have been something bigger than that. And it was! Jesus was talking to religious leaders and pointing out how they were so pure, so
spiritual, and so religious that all they had time to do was
protect their religious proclivities.

The parable was not about doing better. It was about
risk. Given the other stories Jesus told, the company he
kept, and the teaching he gave on mercy, grace, and forgiveness, we can see that the servant who dug a hole and
buried his master's money was admonished because he refused to risk, not because he didn't give a return on the
master's investment. If that servant had received a box of
cigars, a bottle of scotch, and a deck of cards and played
poker with his master's money and lost it all, the master
would not have been displeased!

You can't win in poker or serve Christ courageously
(and with joy) unless you risk. And you can't risk if you
live in fear. Not only that—you will always live in fear if

you aren't covered. That's why having free sins is so very important! In other words, if you serve a hard master, the only thing you can do is dig holes.

Let me show you why Christians should be (even if they aren't) dangerous.

WHAT HAPPENS IF YOU DARE TO BE FREE

1. If you have free sins, you don't have to wear a mask anymore.

I had just come out of the studio where we do our talk show, *Steve Brown Etc.*, and on this particular program we interviewed a friend of mine, Nate Larkin. You can read Nate's story in his book, *Samson and the Pirate Monks: Calling Men to Authentic Brotherhood*. It's a long story and it isn't pretty. Nate was a graduate of Princeton and a successful pastor. He was "Saint Nate." Yet during all that time, he was addicted to pornography and prostitutes. He finally left the ministry. You can only live that kind of double life so long before you are crushed with the burden.

Nate was miserable and lonely and trying to get free. He had moments of freedom but thought that if he could just live the persona of "Saint Nate" all the time, he would be fixed. He tried, but it didn't work. "A false self can never rest. It looks like a real person, but a persona is actually just a hologram, a projected image, and it requires constant energy to keep that image up. A persona is afraid to go to sleep, because to sleep is to die."[2]

You can read the details in the book, but let me tell

you the two things that stood out in the interview. The first was what Nate said and the second was what he did. Nate said that he came to the realization that God didn't love "Saint Nate" and, in fact, didn't even like him, because he had not created "Saint Nate"; he had created Nate. And Nate found out that God loved Nate—the real Nate, the screwed-up Nate, the sinful Nate.

But the second thing that stood out in the interview was Nate's laughter. It was infectious, free, and delightful. I told him that I loved his laughter, and he

> *Nate found out that God loved Nate—the real Nate, the screwed-up Nate, the sinful Nate.*

said it was the laughter of someone who no longer had to pretend, hide, or play a role. It was the laughter of freedom. It makes Nate dangerous.

Jesus said, "Nothing is covered up that will not be revealed, or hidden that will not be known. Therefore whatever you have said in the dark shall be heard in the light, and what you have whispered in private rooms shall be proclaimed on the housetops" (Luke 12:2–3). That always scared me to death when I thought about what I had worked so hard to cover, what I had whispered in private rooms, and what I had said and thought in the dark. Good heavens! The potential shame is crushing.

Well, it's crushing unless I have already revealed the secrets. For much of my life as a professional religionist, I've worked very hard to hide behind the mask of goodness, purity, and religiosity. I finally decided that I just couldn't do it anymore and started telling people the truth. When I did, they smiled and called me "authentic" and "real." Truth is, I'm not authentic and real . . . I'm scared. If I tell you who I really am, you won't be so shocked when you find out.

Any Christian who can't say to those who curse him or her, "You don't know nothin'! If you knew the truth, you would be even more shocked!" hasn't understood what the gospel is about and how freeing it is. There is nothing you can say about me that isn't either true or potentially true. Just writing that sentence gives me incredible freedom and makes me dangerous.

2. If you have free sins, you don't have to please anybody but Jesus.

Having free sins doesn't only mean that you can throw away the mask, it also means that you don't have anybody to please except Jesus—and he's already pleased.

In Acts 4, the disciples are arrested. Luke tells us that the religious leaders saw their boldness and figured they had "been with Jesus." They told the disciples to back off, and the disciples replied, "Whether it is right in the sight of God to listen to you rather than to God, you must judge, for we cannot but speak of what we have seen and heard" (vv. 19–20).

Please note the connection between "being with Jesus" and the disciples' boldness in the face of death and persecution. If Jesus loves you unconditionally and he is pleased, you don't have to give a rip about pleasing anybody else no matter how much power he or she has. That's why Christians can be so dangerous.

3. If you have free sins, you are free from the need to be perfect.

If you have a pile of free sins, not only can you throw away the mask and please only Jesus, who's already pleased, but you are also free from the neurotic need to be perfect.

Scripture says, "There is therefore now no condemnation for those who are in Christ Jesus. For the law of the Spirit of life has set you free in Christ Jesus from the law of sin and death" (Romans 8:1–2). Isaiah the prophet tells us that God said, "Come now, let us reason together, says the LORD: though your sins are like scarlet, they shall be as white as snow; though they are red like crimson, they shall become like wool" (Isaiah 1:18).

If it's already done, why do we keep trying to do it? Because we don't really believe it's done, and this makes us neurotic. A clear indication of this particular neurosis is a bent toward perfectionism. And that perfectionism is so obsessive we hardly have time to do anything but try harder until we get it right. Not only that—a perfectionist works hard at admonishing others to be

> *Perfectionism is so obsessive that we hardly have time to do anything but try harder until we get it right.*

perfect. That causes the perfectionist's sickness, like a cold, to spread its germs everywhere. But that's not the worst part. Our perfectionism doesn't allow us to say what we think, to speak truth that would offend, or to risk anything for the kingdom.

4. If I have free sins, I recognize my value to the One who assigns value.

There is something else important here. If I have free sins, not only do I not have to wear a mask anymore, not have to please anybody but Jesus, and can quit trying to achieve an impossible state of perfection, but I can also begin to recognize my incredible value to the only One who has the right to assign value. With all the humility I can muster, I'm pretty incredible . . . and that makes me dangerous.

Everybody in the world except me has read Rick Warren's book *The Purpose-Driven Life.* I'm sure it's a wonderful book, and I have tremendous respect and admiration for Rick Warren, but I'm simply not reading anything with "purpose" and "driven" in the title. I already have enough trouble getting through the day without screwing it up so badly I can't fix it. I just can't deal with any more.

I do, however, know one statement in the book (because every friend I have has quoted it to me): "It's not about you. It's about God." Okay, I get that. I'm a Presbyterian and know that God is sovereign, I don't get a vote, I don't get to run the universe, and God doesn't need my help.

But in one sense, it really is about me, isn't it? When Moses asked God his name in Exodus 3, God said that he was the great "I AM."

Well, "I am" too. So are you. And not only that, but God has gone to a lot of trouble to show us just how very valuable we are.

In his book *About You*, Dick Staub offers a "creed for the fully human." He writes, "I am a masterpiece, a genius, who, to be satisfied in this life and the next, simply must reach my fullest potential. The glory of God is a human fully alive, and to go to the grave with my song still in me would dishonor my creator and diminish me. I am of great worth. Because I bear a unique imprint of God's image, I possess distinct spiritual, intellectual, creative and relational capacities ready to be developed and expressed. . . . I've come to my senses, I have returned to my creator."[3]

That, of course, is healthy. What isn't healthy is the neurotic, religious focus on becoming valuable and "important to the kingdom."

I have a friend, Wayne Terry, who has Alzheimer's and his book, *Time Zones: Slipping Away*, is a sobering and inspiring story of how Christians deal with the hard things of life.[4] Wayne was recently a guest on our talk show. He said that when he first got the diagnosis, he was horrified and afraid, but then Jesus told him, "I'll walk into the mist with you." Wayne said that Jesus has done that and the experience of the closing mist has been matched with the experience of Christ's presence.

Wayne is working on another book, and I'm praying that he finishes it. The title is wonderful: *I'm Beginning to Miss Me*. There is great pathos in that title . . . and also great freedom.

I'm beginning to miss me, too, and it is a wonderful feeling. I've expended so much effort on being important, respected, and valuable. I've given up trying to be better (it wasn't working anyway), doing it right (I was hitting it about 49 percent of the time, and that was more accidental than anything else), and wanting everybody to be impressed by my faithfulness (they knew the truth but were kind enough not to tell me). I found out that it really isn't about me and my faithfulness, perfection, and obedience. It's about Another, who is perfect in his faithfulness and obedience.

That would be Jesus.

Jesus told me he likes me and that I should go out and play . . . and work and dance and sing and laugh. Jesus said that I could do all of that with the sure confidence that I had all the free sins I would ever need. Jesus said, "Greater love has no one than this, that someone lays down his life for his friends. You are my friends" (John 15:13–14).

I teach seminary students how to talk better. Frankly, that is a difficult task. Public speaking is scary and study after study has shown that almost everybody would rather go to the dentist than speak in front of people. It is one of the major human fears, and that fear is difficult to overcome. A part of my job description is to ameliorate that fear.

There are a number of ways I try to accomplish that task (e.g., practice, techniques for lowering the anxiety level, preparation, etc.), but by far the most helpful thing with the students is to disabuse them of the "Harry and the humble habit," which most of them have acquired in religious circles.

"When you go before a congregation," I tell them, "don't go into a panic and then try to fix it. If you aren't prepared, it's too late to fix it. Prayer doesn't help much either. If you aren't 'prayed up,' it's too late to do that too. Instead, memorize this speech and give it to yourself just before you speak: *I'm the man!* (And yes, I teach women to say that too.) *Get out of the way! I'm God's anointed. I have a message from the High King of Heaven, and he has commissioned me to deliver it. I don't work for you; I work for him. My desire is to please him, not you, and he's already pleased. And by God, I'm going to do what he has told me to do. You may not like it, you may wish I would just go away, and you may choose to ignore it, but you will listen!*"

You ought to hear the students' protests. "Dr. Brown," they say, "that doesn't sound Christian. In fact, it sounds prideful and arrogant. How can I do something that violates my basic beliefs?"

"Your basic beliefs are wrong," I respond, "but nevertheless, do what I say, and God will use you. If you still think it's a sin, repent of it after you get out of the pulpit but not before. Someday when you mature and realize how valuable you are to God, you'll rise up and call me blessed."

People who know they are valuable to God—to the only One who counts—are dangerous. Value comes from the realization that if all my sins are free, I must be privileged royalty.

We are! And because we have unlimited free sins, we're dangerous.

There is a great story about a little boy who killed his grandmother's pet duck.

> *Because we have unlimited free sins, we're dangerous.*

He accidentally hit the duck with a rock from his slingshot. The boy didn't think anybody saw the foul (sorry!) deed, so he buried the duck in the backyard and didn't tell a soul.

Later, the boy found out that his sister had seen it all. And she now had the leverage of his secret and used it. Whenever it was the sister's turn to wash the dishes, take out the garbage, or wash the car, she would whisper in his ear, "Remember the duck." And then the little boy would do whatever his sister should have done.

There is always a limit to that sort of thing. Finally he'd had it. The boy went to his grandmother and, with great fear, confessed what he had done. To his surprise, she hugged him and thanked him. She said, "I was standing at the kitchen sink and saw the whole thing. I forgave you then. I was just wondering when you were going to get tired of your sister's blackmail and come to me."

If you're tired of the manipulation of the duck, you're free. God saw you do it, and you're forgiven. Now you're dangerous.

So go out and offend (or maybe bless or love) someone!

The love of Christ controls us,

because we have concluded this: that one has died for all.

—2 Corinthians 5:14

You have died and your life is hidden with Christ in God.

—Colossians 3:3

7

· · ·

When Getting Better Doesn't Matter

What do you mean? Of course getting better matters!

Okay, so maybe it does, but caring that it does will make you weird. And even if you get better and you know it, you're probably not really getting better. Not only that—if you make getting better your goal, you're in for a boatload of disappointment.

The gospel of free sins makes getting better sort of irrelevant. In fact, the constant pressure to "get better and better, every day in every way" is driving people away from the truth of the gospel. It's not about getting better.

I recently read the books and interviewed some of the authors of *unChristian: What a New Generation Really Thinks about Christianity . . . and Why It Matters*[1] and *The Outsider Interviews: A New Generation Speaks Out on Christianity.*[2] Frankly, I don't care as much as they do about what people think about Christians, but what they found out is interesting.

Let me summarize those books for you in theological language: We Christians are driving people nuts. And maybe more important than that, we're driving ourselves nuts.

I know how to fix it: three free sins!

Let's start with a principle: almost everything of any importance is found while we're headed somewhere else. I know that runs counter to the common wisdom of most leaders, but nevertheless, it's true. We are admonished by almost everybody "who knows" that goals are important and if we don't aim at something, we won't hit anything. "Go for it!" is the mantra of our culture. If you want money, fame, a new car, a better position, a bigger house, or an early retirement, set your goals, focus, commit, and go for it!

While setting goals is a good thing and setting laudable goals even better, if you get neurotic about it, you probably won't achieve your goals, and you'll make yourself and everybody you know miserable in the process. Christians, by and large, are neurotic about purity, obedience, and holiness. It is probably the main reason we're not very pure, obedient, and holy. And in order to maintain our witness, we have learned to fake it.

C. S. Lewis, in a wonderful essay titled "The Inner Ring," which came from a speech given by Lewis to students at the University of London in 1944, says:

> You have met the phenomenon of an Inner Ring. You
> discovered one in your house at school before the

end of the first term. And when you had climbed up to somewhere near it by the end of your second year, perhaps you discovered that within the Ring there was a Ring yet more inner, which in its turn was the fringe of the great school Ring to which the house Rings were only satellites. It is even possible that the School Ring was almost in touch with a Master's Ring. You were beginning, in fact, to pierce through the skins of the onion. And here, too, at your university—shall I be wrong in assuming that at this very moment, invisible to me, there are several rings—independent systems or concentric rings—present in this room? And I can assure you that in whatever hospital, inn of court, diocese, school, business, or college you arrive after going down, you will find the Rings. . . . Of all passions the passion for the Inner Ring is most skilful in making a man who is not yet a very bad man do very bad things.[3]

In other words, intentionally trying to be a part of the in group can mess you up. Lewis then suggests that one should find out what one does well and do it. Then one will find himself or herself in a real inner ring and the only one that matters. Obsessive concern with achieving anything (including being a part of the inner ring) will often be the very thing that assures you won't achieve the object of your obsession.

The book of Ecclesiastes in the Bible is a realistic and, I believe, accurate view of the world as it is—especially when God isn't factored into the equation. The writer of Ecclesiastes has been there, done that, and has several T-shirts. He allows us to see what is important and what isn't. Let me give you a verse from that book: "Whatever your hand finds to do, do it with your might" (9:10). That means your life is too important to waste on trying to do the impossible. Best to do what you're called to do, what you do best, and what is put in front of you. Then the impossible might become possible. In other words, almost everything of any importance is found when you are headed somewhere else, and that includes getting better.

FOUR TRUTHS THAT CAN CHANGE YOUR LIFE

I want to give you four truths that can change your life and maybe even make you better. Then again, maybe not on the "better" part, but that's okay.

1. You don't have to get better.

This first truth is the essence of the gospel and this book. You don't have to get better to get God to love you. You don't have to get better to maintain God's love. You don't have to get better to witness. You don't have to get better to be forgiven. You don't have to get better to "make a difference." And you don't have to get better to be sanctified or holy.

One of the most amazing chapters in the Bible is

Romans 7. The apostle Paul said things that a religious leader shouldn't say if he wants to keep his job! He said, "I do not understand my own actions. For I do not do what I want, but I do the very thing I hate. . . . For I know that nothing good dwells in me, . . . I have the desire to do what is right, but not the ability to carry it out. For I do not do the good I want, but the evil I do not want is what I keep on doing" (vv. 15, 18–19).

The interesting thing about Paul's words is the verb tense. They are present tense and are not a confession of sin whose statute of limitations has long since run out. Paul is talking about the ongoing experience of every Christian and a whole lot of people who aren't.

It's not just Paul and Romans 7 either. Throughout the Bible, God persists in illustrating Paul's words with incredible ruthlessness. Moses was an angry, petulant, and confused leader. Abraham lied in telling the king that his wife was his sister to make her sexually available to him. Abraham also had a sexual relationship with a slave, which, as you can imagine, caused all kinds of problems. Yet Moses and Abraham are our biblical heroes.

The whole superstructure of our Judeo Christian heritage was built on a con game. His name was Jacob and he conned his brother out of his birthright. Jacob is one of our heroes too. David was an adulterer and, not being satisfied with that, arranged to have the husband of the woman with whom he had the affair killed in battle. Jeremiah was consumed with fear. Hosea married a prostitute who refused to be faithful to him and then was used as an example of God's love for his people.

It doesn't get a whole lot better in the New Testament. Paul and Barnabas, early Christian leaders, were on different sides in a church fight that was so big they couldn't even speak to each other or work together. Their first assistant was a coward. We all know about Peter and his denial of Christ, but he didn't become the pristine example of purity after that either. In fact, in the Bible he is referred to as a hypocrite. Peter, Paul, and Barnabas are our heroes too.

It's everywhere! Sometimes I want to tell God that we really do need better heroes than the ones he gave us and that he certainly could have kept some of the family secrets to himself.

Maybe God is trying to communicate something to us.

You think?

One of the most important passages in the Bible is in Genesis 15. It is about a ceremony where God sealed the covenant he had made with Abram (later Abraham).

It's kind of a bloody deal. (Even if contemporary or traditional worship ticks you off, it's still better than killing off a bunch of animals in the sanctuary of the church.) This is how it worked. It was called "cutting a covenant." (We would say "cutting a deal.") The cutting-up part came in cutting animals in half (in this case a heifer, a goat, a ram, a turtledove, and a pigeon) and putting the halves on either side of a path through which the people who were making the covenant/deal walked, thus sealing the deal. Each person had certain obligations or responsibilities and got a certain return. The symbolism of the whole process suggested that those who "cut the covenant" as they walked down the path between the two halves were saying, "If I don't fulfill my side of this covenant, may the same thing that happened to these animals happen to me."

Abram then went into a deep sleep, and the text reads, "When the sun had gone down and it was dark, behold, a smoking fire pot and a flaming torch passed between these pieces. On that day the Lord made a covenant with Abram, saying, 'To your offspring I give this land, from the river of Egypt to the great river, the river Euphrates'" (vv. 17–18).

The interesting thing about this particular "cutting of the covenant" is that Abram didn't walk through the pieces of cut-up animals. The truly amazing thing about the whole incident is that it was God—and God alone— who walked down the path between the cut-up animals. God was saying that Abram wasn't required to *do* anything, to obey the laws of the covenant, to be faithful, or anything else. That was God's business; he would fulfill all the requirements and obligations of the covenant!

That, of course, was the beginning of the story (a shadow, if you will) that has an incredible climax on a cross where God came and covered every requirement of the covenant with the blood of his own Son. During the

Reformation when Luther said that the only thing he brought to his salvation was his sin and his reluctance, he articulated the amazing message of the Christian faith—God did all the fulfilling that needed fulfilling, and that means we don't have to fulfill anything.

2. You will get better, and you won't be able to help it.

Paul wrote to the Philippians, "I am sure of this, that he who began a good work in you will bring it to completion at the day of Jesus Christ" (Philippians 1:6). The apostle John adds his affirmation, "Beloved, we are God's children now, and what we will be has not yet appeared; but we know that when he appears we shall be like him" (1 John 3:2).

Quietism is a very old Christian heresy founded by an old, dead white guy named Miguel de Molinos. (It's also, just to impress you with my knowledge, a philosophy taught by another old, dead white guy named Ludwig Wittgenstein, but that's something else.) Quietism suggests that you do nothing except "annihilate yourself" and God does the rest.

The Christian faith has never been quietist. "Go," "speak," "defend," "fight," "do," etc. are words found throughout the Bible. I wouldn't suggest that you just sit around doing nothing. Rather let me suggest that you do something (preferably something you like, are good at, and which doesn't cause more damage than you can fix) and "let the devil take the hindmost." I promise that you will one day wake up and find that you "smell like Jesus." You will find yourself better than you were. It's the promise of God and the experience of every believer who refused to get neurotic about his or her own goodness and obedience.

Someone has suggested that when you come running to God, he gives you a mirror and a picture of Jesus. God

> *I promise that you will one day wake up and find that you "smell like Jesus."*

says, "Look in the mirror, and then look at the picture. As we walk together, you are going to change from what you are to what he is. Meanwhile, go on about your business and let me walk with you."

I have the mother of all lemon trees in my backyard. In fact, my neighbors often comment about the magnificence of that tree and its fruit. The lemons don't even look like lemons; they look like grapefruit but are often bigger than grapefruit. That's not all. There are hundreds of lemons on that tree every year. We give them to family and friends and leave a few for the squirrels and mice who, for some reason, like lemons. It really is an incredible tree.

Do you know what I did to get that tree to have lemons? Absolutely nothing. I didn't water it, I didn't fertilize it, and I didn't talk to it. The truth is that I'm not big on lemons, and it would be perfectly fine with me if the tree were to die. I almost cut it down on a couple of occasions.

We had no lemons for the first two full years. There were times when that tree looked like it wasn't even trying. Once, with the exception of a few scattered leaves, it looked like it had died. No fruit and no life. If I had had Jesus' powers, I would have cursed that lemon tree (as Jesus did with the fig tree in Matthew 21) and watched it die. I actually planned to plant an orange tree in the place of that lemon tree because I like oranges better than lemons.

Then the third year, there were a couple of lemons on the tree. The next year, a few more. And by the next, there were more lemons than I could handle.

Donald Grey Barnhouse—the late, much lauded Bible teacher and pastor at Tenth Presbyterian Church in Philadelphia—said that all of life illustrates biblical doctrine. My lemon tree is one of those illustrations. The lemon tree didn't grunt and try really hard to have lemons. The tree is a lemon tree and lemon trees have lemons. To mix the metaphor, dogs don't bark to become dogs; they bark because they are dogs.

The Bible says that if we are in Christ, we are new creations. "The old has passed away; behold, the new has come" (2 Corinthians 5:17).

But it becomes a problem when we turn that fact into a commandment. Paul isn't saying that we should *do* anything. He is telling us who we are. You don't have to work, be more religious, be pure enough for unbelievers to notice, read the Bible, or pray to become a new creation—that is what you already are. And for the rest of your life he will work in you to make you like Jesus.

What God starts, he always finishes. The very fact that he started his work in you is an absolute promise that you will be completed . . . so lighten up and go live your life.

3. If you get better, hardly anybody will know.

Of course we are to recognize that, as Jesus said, bad fruit comes from bad trees and good fruit comes from good trees. We are to pursue the "fruit of the Spirit" in our lives (love, joy, peace, patience, kindness, goodness, faithfulness, gentleness, and self-control, from Galatians 5:22–23), but the problem with all of that is that it can be so easily faked.

Have you ever noticed the news reports following the apprehension of a serial killer? Almost without exception, people who are interviewed say that the killer was a quiet sort, pretty much kept to himself, seemed like a nice man, and liked kittens and children. Obviously, something was going on that nobody recognized.

There is always something going on in every life that others don't know about. After listening to confessions for most of my professional life, I have a couple of reactions to those confessions. The first is an awareness that the people to whom I listened were just like me. The second reaction is always: "I didn't know that about you and never would have known if you had not told me."

In fact, if you're reading this book and want to have

some good friendships among believers, want to go to our parties and share in our fun but can't buy into all the stuff about Jesus, I can help. First, if you're reading this book, you're out of your mind. And second, you can learn to fake it so that nobody will know. I can teach you a few words that you must use, I can help you look the way you ought to look, and I can show you the minefields to avoid and the places to affirm. In fact, I can show you how to be so phony that nobody will ever know.

One time Mr. and Mrs. Billy Graham were in church together, and Mr. Graham, by mistake, put a twenty-dollar bill in the collection plate when he meant to give a ten. He reached for the twenty-dollar bill, and Mrs. Graham slapped his hand. "I meant," he whispered, "to put a ten-dollar bill in the offering."

"In God's eyes," Mrs. Graham quietly assured him, "it's a ten."

Jesus said some radical things; one of the most radical you'll find (at least for this preacher) is in his Sermon on the Mount. He said, "Beware of practicing your righteousness before other people in order to be seen by them, for then you will have no reward from your Father who is in heaven" (Matthew 6:1). Later in that chapter, he said this: "And when you fast, do not look gloomy like the hypocrites, for they disfigure their faces that their fasting may be seen by others. Truly I say to you, they have received their reward" (v. 16). Jesus didn't stop there. He said in

Matthew 7:22–23, "On that day many will say to me, 'Lord, Lord, did we not prophesy in your name, and cast out demons in your name, and do many mighty works in your name?' And then will I declare to them, 'I never knew you; depart from me.'"

Goodness is easy to fake, and when people affirm your apparent goodness, two things happen. First, the feeling you have about your own righteousness will establish a pattern that will spiral upward (or downward) to cause the false mask you wear to be even more real than who you really are.

And second, God will notice.

I recently had lunch with a number of Christian counselors. My friend, who is the head of the clinic, set it up because he wanted to give the counselors some time with me to ask questions and to talk about vision. The problem with my friend is that we have walked together a long time and, on one occasion, I stood with him when others wouldn't. He calls me his "father in the faith." As a result, he has far too high an opinion of me. To make it worse, he had shared that too-high opinion with his coworkers, and even worse, they believed him.

You should have been there! They repeatedly told me how amazed they were that I would take time from my busy schedule to spend it with them. When I said things (and some of the things I said were really dumb), they listened, took notes, and seemed to think that I was speaking from Sinai. I loved those counselors for their authenticity and their affirmation. But what I loved best was that they thought so highly of me.

As I drove away from that lunch, thinking how fortunate they had been to spend time with me, I heard laughter. It was the laughter of the angels. I actually thought, *Wonder how often those counselors have been with one so wise and profound?* And God said, *One less time than you think.*

Think of the most obedient, wonderful, faithful, and holy Christian you know in your church. Now listen. If he got drunk at a Christian party and confessed his deepest and darkest secrets, you would be shocked. Now look around your community on the streets that run by the church. If you picked someone at random and looked into his or her heart, you might substitute that person for the "saint" you just lost in church.

4. If you do get better, you probably won't even know it.

There is a delightful story in 1 Samuel 9–10 where Saul is chosen to be the king over God's people. I'll make a fairly long story short. It started with lost donkeys. Saul's father had lost some donkeys and sent Saul to find them. Saul couldn't find the donkeys and decided to go home before his father stopped worrying about the donkeys and started worrying about him. But Saul's servant told Saul that a "man of God" by the name of Samuel was in the area and wondered if perhaps this man could help find the donkeys.

Unbeknownst to Saul, God had told Samuel that he would show him who was to be the first king of Israel. When Saul approached Samuel to get his help with the donkeys, God told Samuel that Saul was the man. Samuel then began to inform a very surprised and confused Saul of that fact, and Saul replied, "Am I not a Benjaminite, from the least of the tribes of Israel? And is not my clan the humblest of all the clans of the tribe of Benjamin? Why then have you spoken to me in this way?" (9:21). Even after Samuel anointed Saul as king of Israel and Saul went home, he was reticent about telling his family that he was now the king.

(In case you were wondering, God found the donkeys for Saul's father.)

My late mentor, Fred Smith, used to tell a story about a corporation head or some other highly regarded leader— I would tell you the man's name and more details if I could ask Fred, but Fred is in heaven and won't talk to me—who was honored at a dinner. It was to be a surprise. After the food was served and consumed, the emcee came to the microphone and announced that the dinner was a surprise award dinner. The emcee named the one to be honored. Everybody stood and started applauding. Fred said he looked over and noticed that the man who was being honored was standing and applauding too. Fred would laugh and say, "Even after they told him about the honor, he thought it was for someone else."

Isaiah the prophet tells us that God said, "I dwell in the

high and holy place, and also with him who is of a contrite and lowly spirit, to revive the spirit of the lowly, and to revive the heart of the contrite" (57:15). You may also remember Jesus said that God affirmed and justified the tax collector (a great sinner) when he prayed and, at the same time, did not justify and affirm the Pharisee who was a "religious professional" and had done a whole lot of good and righteous works.

There are a number of passages in the New Testament from which teachers draw the doctrine of crowns. It's the suggestion that while we get to heaven by grace, not everybody is going to have *earned* crowns. When we get there, those who have been especially good, faithful, pure, and obedient will be awarded crowns. And there will be great affirmation of those who have earned those crowns. Then the really spiritual ones will, as a hymn suggests, "lay their crowns at Jesus' feet."

Okay. Maybe.

I believe that teaching violates the thrust of the Bible and the gospel and there is another way to look at it. That's for another book, but let me tell you one thing for sure. If some of us do get crowns in heaven, we'll be surprised by who gets them and the people who receive them will be the most surprised of all.

Let me give you a principle: The closer you get to God, the better you are at serving him. And the more you are sanctified, the less you will *feel* close to God or that you are serving well and that you are, as John Wesley (the founder of Methodism) said, "moving on to perfection."

One of the questions asked of those being ordained in the Methodist Church (I was ordained a Methodist minister) is this: are you moving on to perfection?

When I was asked that question, I thought about it and decided that I might not be a very good and spiritual person, but I was, after all, being ordained and that made me somewhat better than most others. I figured that I was "moving on to perfection" . . . at least sort of. So I answered *yes*.

I was very young then and now I'm old as dirt. Over the years, God has granted me the severe mercy of failure, pain, and an awareness of how I'm about as messed up as anybody I know. If I were asked that question again, I would have to answer that I hoped maybe I was getting better. "But frankly," I would have to say, "who the hell knows?"

> God has granted me the severe mercy of failure, pain, and an awareness of how I'm about as messed up as anybody I know.

There is a degree of comfort in that attitude because maybe I am better simply because I'm not sure. Then again, maybe I'm really not better.

Either way, it doesn't matter, because that isn't the issue. Jesus loves me big either way!

You too!

Now if what I've taught you in this chapter is true (and it is)—you don't have to get better, you will get better anyway, and you and others won't know if you do get better—how does that apply to our lives with Christ?

It means that you can go on about your life without all the religious obsession over your own purity and goodness. Nobody cares whether you're good or not, and while God cares, he doesn't obsess over your goodness. He did something about it. God forgave you when you didn't deserve it, and he gave you the righteousness of his Son. You're fixed, and you probably didn't even know it.

Now you do!

Isn't that a relief?

You did not receive the spirit of slavery

to fall back into fear,

but you have received the Spirit of adoption as sons,

by whom we cry "Abba! Father!"

—Romans 8:15

Since we have a great priest over the house of God,

let us draw near.

—Hebrews 10:21–22

8
. . .
The Other Side of Silence

Pascal, the sixteenth-century scientist, philosopher, and theologian, said, "The eternal silence of these infinite spaces frightens me."[1] George Eliot, the nineteenth-century Victorian novelist, referenced in her novel *Middlemarch* the silence of the grass growing and the heartbeat of a squirrel. She wrote that if we could really hear, we would be frightened by the "roar" on the "other side of the silence."

I get that.

You do too!

It's why we don't pray much. We're afraid. The atheist is afraid that God might show. That's a pretty scary thought. Atheists must be very careful about thinking too much, reading the wrong books, befriending the wrong people, and certainly about being quiet. What if God should show? If he did, God would be in charge and—if autonomy is the issue—people could lose their power. If I were an atheist, I would keep moving too . . . because the Hound of Heaven might be gaining on me.

But I'm not so much concerned here with the silence that scares unbelievers. I'm concerned with the silence that scares most of us who do believe. In that silence, there is the frightening thought that nobody is there or, if there is somebody there, he is not altogether happy with us and we will get what we deserve. So we do religious things, talk religious talk, and go to religious meetings. We keep busy doing God stuff lest we get quiet and have the same Hound of Heaven show up and destroy us.

If you don't pray much, and if what's on the other side of silence is worrisome to you, I'm here to help.

I've checked. On the other side of silence, there is a great and wonderful surprise, but you can't get there from here without three free sins. I'm going to show you, but it will take a bit, so bear with me.

I'm a man of prayer!

That sounds so pious. As I wrote that, I winced. Nevertheless, it's true. I get up quite early each morning and spend a considerable time in prayer. Coffee and Jesus (not necessarily in that order) wake me up when most of you are still in bed. Sometimes I'm on my knees, and at other times I'm prostrate on the floor before God. Sometimes I use the liturgy from the Church of Scotland's *Book of Common Order* (*Worship*) or read from Thomas à Kempis or the Puritans. I worship God and, in doing it, have this sense that this is why I was created. Not only that. I bring to him every need and every problem, trusting him with it all. I pray for a whole lot of people I care about and do it daily, seeing God do some amazing things. It's a wonderful time!

Wait!

There are other times when I "cuss and spit," when God seems to have taken a vacation to Bermuda and when I play solitaire on my computer instead of praying. Sometimes I tell God what I really think about him and how he runs his universe (not altogether very spiritual comments). I tell him how upset I am about what he's done to people I love. Sometimes I'm just ticked at life in general and have a pity party before God's throne. There are times when I feel so guilty I can hardly breathe (that's because I really am that guilty and have messed up some important areas of my life), and other times when I try to make excuses and rationalize my sin and the people I've hurt. Other times I pray that some people I don't like get the hives. There are times when I doubt, and there are times when I feel so alone and afraid that I think I'm not going to pray anymore.

If that confuses you, I understand. In fact, you probably think I ought to be careful in thunderstorms.

I'm not, and therein lies one of the most exciting and

> *Sometimes I tell God what I really think about him and how he runs his universe (not altogether very spiritual comments).*

fundamental elements of recognizing that the essence of the Christian faith is the redemption that provides free sins. On the other side of silence isn't the roar that frightens you or the emptiness that keeps you awake at night. On the other side of silence there isn't a child abuser who will break your legs if you get out of line or a policeman with a big stick.

On the other side of silence is your Father . . . a good Father the Bible says we can call "Daddy." On the other side of silence is a place where your goodness, your obedience, your fear, and your trying harder is no longer the issue. On the other side of silence is a soft place where there is intimacy, love, and acceptance.

If you really believed this were true, you might become a woman or man of prayer too.

WHY WE DON'T PRAY

There are a number of reasons we don't pray much. And even when we do, prayer is not an altogether positive or pleasant experience.

1. We don't pray because we feel intimidated.

The first reason we don't pray is because we're dealing with the intimidation factor (or as R. C. Sproul calls it, "cosmic claustrophobia"). God is big and scary. God says in Scripture, "My thoughts are not your thoughts, neither are your ways my ways. . . . For as the heavens are higher than the earth, so are my ways higher than your ways and my thoughts than your thoughts" (Isaiah 55:8–9). It really is a "fearful thing to fall into the hands of the living God" (Hebrews 10:31). The real God is real scary.

As I write this, I have an appointment this afternoon to meet with the new president of Reformed Theological Seminary in Orlando, Dr. Don Sweeting. I suspect that Don likes to meet with me

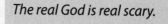

The real God is real scary.

because I'm a "cynical old preacher" who knows how power works, where the minefields are, and the "tricks of the trade" of the seminary corporate culture. He knows that I'm for him in a big way. I'm emeritus at the seminary, so I don't have to go to faculty meetings or serve on committees and I don't have to work with uptight, anal accrediting people. I still teach four or five modular courses each year, but I don't even have to do that if I don't want to. I already have more bubble gum that I can chew, and frankly I don't need the job.

While Don is my friend and I like him a lot, he is also quite intimidating. He is an incredible scholar and I'm not (my doctorates are phony). He was a successful pastor of a large church, and I did the best I could in the smaller churches I served. (While I wasn't half bad at it, sometimes I would like to go back and apologize for some of the things I did as a pastor.) He is focused, gifted, articulate, and very bright; and I'm doing the best I can.

I'm kind of looking forward to my time with Don, but I

also feel a bit uncomfortable. He could fire me anytime he wanted to, and while I don't need the job, it really wouldn't look good on my record. He may have found out some dirt on me and realized that the idea of my being a professor in his institution is insane. He may have heard from students who don't like me and have threatened to leave the seminary if I don't straighten up. Could be that I'm going to get dressed down for a great variety of issues I don't want to go into with you.

So while the thought of meeting with Don is pleasant, there is also a side to the meeting that is quite uncomfortable.

Steve, that's neurotic.

I know it. But it really isn't any more neurotic than how most of us feel when we meet with God. The only difference is that the intimidation factor in our relationship and walk with God is a thousand times bigger and the meeting a thousand times more uncomfortable.

2. He knows all our secrets.

Another reason we don't pray much is because we know that he knows. Scripture says that what God has chosen to reveal to us about himself and the world is a gift he has given to us and our children, but that "the secret things belong to the LORD our God" (Deuteronomy 29:29). I'm taking that verse out of context, but I do assume that the "secret things" include my secrets too.

The psalmist prayed, "Search me, O God, and know my heart! Try me and know my thoughts!" (Psalm 139:23). That sounds like a laudable prayer until you think about it. Then you realize that it is a lot harder than it sounds to pray and to mean it when you do so.

You've probably heard about the drunk with the long-suffering wife who tried to get him sober for years. Finally, in a drunken stupor, he told his wife to pray for him. Grasping the opportunity, she got on her knees and prayed, "Dear Lord, I love my husband but he's drunk . . ."

At that moment, she felt her husband pulling on her sleeve. "Don't tell him I'm drunk," he said, "tell him I'm sick!"

It is not an altogether pleasant task to spend time with someone you can't con or manipulate. God knows it all. If you tell him that you love him when you don't, that you'll serve him when you know it's a lie, or that you'll trust him when you would rather trust a drunken sailor, he will laugh at you. If you don't cuss in his presence but think cuss words, if you're bored out of your skull and pretend that you're not, and if you try to play the religious game with him when he knows the truth, Jesus is going to leave the building. In your heart you know it's true. And it makes prayer an iffy prospect.

> *It is not an altogether pleasant task to spend time with someone you can't con or manipulate.*

3. We really don't trust God.

Another reason we don't pray much is that we really don't trust God. Isaiah the prophet prayed, "Behold, God is my salvation; I will trust, and will not be afraid; for the LORD GOD is my strength and my song, and he has become my salvation" (Isaiah 12:2). Okay, Isaiah was a prophet and I'm not. I'm ordained (that makes me quite religious, more than many of you), but it's still hard for me to trust God all that much. I've watched how he treated some others who loved him more than I do, and it doesn't give me a lot of confidence. St. Teresa is said to have told God that he would have more friends if he treated the ones he had better. Good point, that.

George Bingham is my beloved friend and heads up Key Life. We've been friends for a very long time and trust each other. When the position of CEO opened up at Key Life, I asked George—who had run a large medical company, has an MBA (he's now working on a doctorate), and did consulting for some businesses—if he would pray about moving to Orlando and working with me. I honestly didn't think there was a chance of a snowball in a hot place that he would agree. He did, however, say that he would pray about it. He did, and God told him to come. So George left his job and moved his family to Orlando to manage Key Life.

There is a lot of history in our relationship. George and his wife, Ruth, were members of a church where I served as the pastor. George was an elder, and Ruth was a member of my church staff. They met there, and I had the privilege of performing their marriage ceremony. Early on in their marriage, their eighteen-month-old son, Matthew, died. It's a long and sad story, but during that time, our relationship became far deeper than it had ever been. When Matthew was in the hospital close to death, George and I were walking around, and he said to me, "Steve, people have told me that if Matthew dies, a lot of people will find Christ. Frankly, I would rather they go to hell."

A few years later, we did a promotional video for Key Life, and George and Ruth consented to be a part of that. It was very difficult for them to be in front of the cameras telling the story of Matthew. After it was over, Ruth looked at me and said, with tears streaming down her face, "That was hell, and we wouldn't do that for anybody but you." Then Ruth said to me, "Do you know the hardest thing about Matthew's death?" I allowed that I didn't, and she said, "The hardest thing about Matthew's death is trusting God again. I will serve him because he's God, but I'm not sure that I will ever be able to trust him."

Charles Spurgeon said that when we can't "trace God's hand" we should "trust his heart." Ruth and George know that now, and slowly (not perfectly) their trust of God has come back. But it was a hard road getting there. And if you don't understand that, you have never thought very deeply about why really bad things happen to good people.

4. Our guilt prevents us from praying.

By far, though, the most salient reason we don't pray much is our guilt. David cried out to God after his sin of murder and adultery, "I know my transgressions, and my sin is ever before me. Against you, you only, have I sinned and done what is evil in your sight, so that you may be justified in your words and blameless in your judgment" (Psalm 51:3–4).

Okay, the odds are that you've never committed murder, but unless you are an unusually passive personality, you've thought about it. And if you didn't do it, you maybe prayed for someone's death. And if you didn't do that, there is a good chance that if that person did assume room temperature, you wouldn't be altogether bereft. If you would never commit adultery, you've probably thought about it. Jesus said in Matthew 5:28 that a "benign" bit of "lustful intent" means you're guilty of the real thing. So your name is David.

Even if your name isn't David, you have your own stuff, too, and it isn't very pretty. When Paul made his great confession, he cried out with the same words every thinking believer cries, "Wretched man that I am! Who will deliver me from this body of death?" (Romans 7:24). If you can't identify with that, you're crazy for having read this far in the book.

I recently got an email from a man who told me his secrets. I'm not sure why people do that. Maybe they identify with the doctor who told me that most of his life he had listened to preachers and missionaries saying that they were sinners. "But you're the first one," he said, "that I ever believed." For whatever reason, this man confessed some very dark stuff he had done a long time ago—before he had been part of a church, involved in its programs, and even led others to Christ.

He wrote: *I can't believe that I'm telling you this. What do you think? You talk about God not being angry, but I would be. In fact, I would be very angry at me; and I don't think, if I were God, I would have anything to do with me.*

I wrote back that God told me to tell him to "come on home."

You didn't!

Yes, I did, and you need to hear it too!

If you're intimidated by God because he's infinite, big, and eternal and you're finite, little, and going to die; if you wince because he knows all your secrets and can't be conned; if there is no way you can trust the God of earthquakes, tornados, and cancer; and if you simply can't believe that God would have anything to do with you . . . I've got some incredibly good news for you.

Yeah, you guessed it: three free sins!

I once interviewed Anne Lamott, the award-winning novelist and writer, for our talk show. It was a phone interview that didn't start well. She was late for an appointment and had had a bad experience with an airline, so the last thing she wanted to do was talk to me. "Can we keep this short?" she asked, and I told her that we would.

"But before we start," I said, "let me ask you something. Do you know those right-wing fundy preachers who don't like you and criticize you so harshly?" Anne allowed that she did. "Well," I went on, "I'm one of them, but before you hang up, I do want you to know that I've just read your book *Traveling Mercies*, and I loved it. And I've probably sold more of that book than you have. Thought you ought to know."

Authors like people who like their work (I know I do). We ended up talking for over an hour. Toward the end of the interview, Anne asked me, "Steve, do you know what we would do if we ever met?" I said that I wasn't sure. "We would," she said, laughing, "hold hands and tell each other stories about Jesus."

I don't agree with Anne Lamott about much except Jesus. But we share a secret that I want to share with you. God isn't the God they told you about. He isn't out to destroy you, demean you, embarrass you, or kick you out. Jesus went to a lot of trouble to give us stories that are surprising and profound. Those are stories of love, joy, and welcome.

> *"Steve, do you know what we would do if we ever met? We would hold hands and tell each other stories about Jesus."*
> —Anne Lamott

Are you sure?

Yeah, I'm sure. I've gone to the other side of silence and checked it out, and he told me to tell you. On the other side of silence you'll find the surprising reality that

God created you to be his child, his friend, and his own. Augustine was right. God created us for himself, and our hearts really are restless until they find their rest in him.

I want to take a little time to show you the methodology of a God who likes you.

THE REAL GOD

Of course we're intimidated by God. Are you crazy? If you've never stood before God and been terribly afraid, you've never stood before the real God. You created a god of your own liking, an idol-god who simply doesn't exist. Frankly, if I were creating a god and a religion to worship him, it wouldn't be the one in the Bible. I would create a safer deity who was a lot nicer and a whole lot more manageable. God—the real God—is too much!

Isaiah the prophet, who was probably in the church building whistling a contemporary Jewish song when he met the real God, could tell us a thing or two. You can read about the whole incident in Isaiah 6. The real God is not the god Freud said we created (Freud was a twit!). When the real God came, there were gigantic heavenly creatures, smoke, and fire; and the church shook to the foundations. When Isaiah saw God on the throne, his response was, "Oops." Well, not really. He said, "Woe is me! For I am lost; for I am a man of unclean lips, and I dwell in the midst of a people of unclean lips; for my eyes have seen the King, the LORD of hosts!" (6:5).

Now put yourself (a highly presumptuous thought) in the place of an eternal, infinite, omnipotent, omnipresent, omniscient, immutable, sovereign, and awesome God. Further, assume that you, for some strange reason, love the human beings you created and want to reach out to them, love them, have a relationship with them, letting them know about your intentions for them. How would you go about it? You couldn't become something you weren't. And there is no way you could scare them into love. It doesn't work that way. If you're bigger than I am, you can make me do what you want me to do, and if you're big enough, you can even make me smile while I'm doing it . . . but there is no way you can make me love you.

So what do you do?

I have a very deep voice and I'm quite opinionated. Add to that the fact I'm a "religious professional" with all that involves, and I have a problem. An associate once told me, "Steve, when people meet with you, you have to back off, speak softer, and be a little nicer. You're scaring people." I was quite surprised . . . I thought I was warm, kind, and lovable. God is never surprised by who he is. In fact, all of creation is an effort by the Creator to reveal who he is. God is never surprised, either, at how intimidating he can be. He created us and he knows.

But he still has a problem.

God's problem is kind of like the one faced by the farmer who, in a snowstorm, tried to get the cold and starving birds to come into his barn. But all he did was frighten them, and they died.

But there are descriptions of God as *Father* in the Old Testament and a whole lot of indications that maybe, just maybe, God could be kind and merciful. But then there's also the smoke and the fire. It's kind of like Luke Skywalker finding out that Darth Vader was his father at the end of *The Empire Strikes Back.* That's not necessarily information you want to hear. There are all kinds of fathers, and, frankly, being disowned by some of them would be a favor.

What God did was so incredible and unbelievable that it takes your breath away.

"Long ago, at many times and in many ways, God spoke to our fathers by the prophets, but in these last days he has spoken to us by his Son, whom he appointed the heir of all things" (Hebrews 1:1–2). John wrote, "In the beginning was the Word, and the Word was with God, and the Word was God. . . . And the Word became flesh and dwelt among us. . . . And from his fullness we have all received, grace upon grace. For the law was given through Moses; grace and truth came through Jesus Christ (John 1:1, 14, 16–17).

In other words, God set aside the smoke and the thunder, and he whispered so he wouldn't scare the spit out of us. Who would have believed a baby, a stable, and shepherds? Who could have known?

Okay, what does this have to do with the other side of silence? How does this get us there without being killed?

You want to know what God is like? We have to look at Jesus or we'll never understand. In the book of Romans, Paul wrote, "For while we were still weak, at the right time Christ died for the ungodly" (5:6). Again, "There is therefore now no condemnation for those who are in Christ Jesus" (8:1). One more: "If God is for us, who can be against us? He who did not spare his own Son but gave him up for us all, how will he not also with him graciously give us all things? Who shall bring any charge against God's elect? It is God who justifies. Who is to condemn?" (8:31–34).

It's three free sins! No, it's unlimited free sins. Wait, sin isn't even the issue anymore, and that fact opens a door through which we can run to him without getting killed by a holy God.

> *Sin isn't even the issue anymore, and that fact opens a door through which we can run to him without getting killed by a holy God.*

I don't know about you, but I've tried so hard to do this religious thing. I've probably put more effort into it than you have. If you found out that all of it wasn't true, you could try Wicca or start your own religious or agnostic movement. I've put *all* my eggs in this basket and don't have anywhere else to go.

So I worked at it really hard . . . harder than most. I prayed for hours . . . longer than most. I studied the Bible—even getting an academic degree in the subject— far more than most. I tried really hard to be good and faithful. I even tried to be nice. And then I realized I can't do this anymore. I turned and headed out into the cold darkness. I was sadder and wiser.

If you think the Bible is unrealistic and shallow, let me give you some words from Scripture in Ecclesiastes to put in your pipe and smoke. It reflects the efforts of someone (like me and probably you too) who works hard at knowing God:

> Vanity of vanities, says the Preacher, vanity of vanities! All is vanity. . . . I have seen everything that is done under the sun, and behold, all is vanity. . . . What happens to the fool will happen to me also. Why then have I been so very wise? And I said in my heart that this also is vanity. . . . For what happens to the children of man and what happens to the beasts is the same; as one dies, so dies the other. They all have the same breath, and man has no advantage over the beasts, for all is vanity. . . . So I hated life, because what is done under the sun was grievous to me, for all is vanity and a striving after wind. (Ecclesiastes 1:2, 14; 2:15; 3:19; 2:17)

Just when the dark engulfed me, I heard the voice. It was the voice that Jesus—because of his unconditional forgiveness—let me hear.

The voice came from the throne:

"Welcome, child. Welcome."

I came running, and that's how I became a man of prayer.

Be sober-minded; be watchful.

Your adversary the devil prowls around like a roaring lion,

seeking someone to devour.

—1 Peter 5:8

Simon, Simon, behold, Satan demanded to have you,

that he might sift you like wheat,

but I have prayed for you.

—Luke 22:31–32

9

• • •

The Devil Made Me Do It!

I know, I know. But sometimes it really is the devil. Not the one in the red suit with a tail and a pitchfork. The real devil who looks so together, sophisticated, and charming.

THE TRUTH ABOUT SATAN

At the start, I want to give you three truths to lay the foundation for some important biblical instruction on discerning Satan's displeasure at anybody who would suggest that "three free sins" is a part of God's gift to his people.

1. Evil is real, and Satan is alive and well.

C. S. Lewis wrote in the preface to *The Screwtape Letters*:

There are two equal and opposite errors into which our race can fall about the devils. One is to disbelieve in their existence. The other is to believe, and to feel an excessive and unhealthy interest in them. They themselves are equally pleased by both errors and hail a materialist or a magician with the same delight. The sort of script which is used in this book can be very easily obtained by anyone who has once learned the knack; but ill-disposed or excitable people who might make a bad use of it shall not learn it from me.[1]

We didn't get our ideas about Satan from some backwoods, unsophisticated preacher but from Scripture in general and Jesus in particular. Jesus warned Peter about Satan's power (see Luke 22:31). Peter himself warned those to whom he wrote of Satan's power (see 1 Peter 5:8). Neither was talking about a paper tiger. They were letting us know that Satan is real, big, and scary.

When I was a pastor, I had a major problem with people who saw demons under every bed, around every corner, and in every situation. Those people caused some serious problems in the church. In an effort to remedy the situation (the Bible says that bad stuff comes from the world, the flesh, *and* the devil), I said from the pulpit, "Some of you guys are looking for demons everywhere and have made that your focus. It's making you weird, and it's scaring some new Christians in this church. So stop. One of these days you're going to meet the real thing, and he's going to scare the spit out of you." (Just so you know, a number of those people left the church over what I said, and the church was better for it.)

I have a problem with those who give Satan land that doesn't belong to him. But it is also a problem to pretend that evil isn't real and that Satan is only an effort to explain bad stuff in a less sophisticated age.

There was a time in my more theologically liberal days (I was theologically just left of whacko and thought I was an intellectual) when I found it difficult, if not impossible, to refer to the devil or Satan without adding an addendum to the effect that the devil was, of course, the "metaphorical personification of evil."

I'm a lot older now and a bit wiser. I know that those people who left the church over what I said made a serious error in their thinking about Satan. But I did the same thing . . . just in the other direction.

I've seen Satan in demon possession in the Third World and Miami; in the unexplained addictive power of drugs and porn; and in the drawn faces of the hungry and in the pain of the oppressed. Intellectually, Satan partially explains the mystery of evil; and emotionally, he explains some of my own failure and sin. He makes life cheap, purpose meaningless, and values worthless. I've seen Satan, and, frankly, it's an intimidating and scary experience.

> *I've seen Satan, and, frankly, it's an intimidating and scary experience.*

2. Satan is a defeated enemy.

In the words of Martin Luther's famous hymn, "A Mighty Fortress Is Our God," Satan's "doom is sure." The writer of the book of Hebrews said that when Jesus was crucified on the cross, Satan was destroyed (see Hebrews 2:14–15). Paul said about Satan that Jesus shamed and triumphed over him and his authority (see Colossians 2:15).

I have read J. R. R. Tolkien's The Lord of the Rings trilogy and enjoyed Peter Jackson's wonderful film adaptation of those stories more than once. I know the story and how it ends. I know what Frodo goes through to destroy the ring and thus destroy the Dark Lord who is evil beyond imagining. Every time I read the books or watch the films, I wince at the battles, cringe at the death and devastation, and cheer for the good guys . . . even when it looks like all is lost. Each time, though, I know how it ends. I love the final pitch of the ring into the fire and the defeat of the Dark Lord. No matter how scary the journey is, the end is settled. Frodo wins.

Something like that has happened with Satan. The story has been written and the conclusion is settled. In the meanwhile, it can be a rough ride to the conclusion, but the conclusion is already written and complete. Jesus has won and Satan has lost. As someone has said, "The dragon has been slain, but his tail still swishes."

· · ·

3. If you belong to Christ, Satan has no ultimate power over you.

You can't "sell your soul" to the devil; you can't be defeated by him; you can't be destroyed by him; you can't be robbed by him of anything of ultimate importance. First John 4:4 says that the power (the Holy Spirit), which became resident in you and which was given to you when you came running to Jesus, is greater than Satan's power against you.

I remember the first time I ever confronted a bully and won the fight. It was in grade school. I really didn't think I had the power to do anything, but I was tired of his intimidation and derision and finally decided that I wasn't going to take it anymore. So I called out the bully, fully expecting to die. And then, as the fight commenced, I remember wondering who would get my bicycle. I don't remember much of that fight, but I do remember sitting on top of the bully, beating the snot out of him as he cried for me to leave him alone.

And I remember how I felt when the fight was over. I felt free and empowered.

You are free and empowered. Satan doesn't have any power over you. He is God's lackey (see Job 1) and is around for God's reasons and to accomplish God's plan. When the show is over, Satan will be nothing, and all that he tried to destroy will be restored.

One of my friends asked a retired, old preacher about

heaven. The preacher told my friend that the best thing about heaven would be watching Jesus pick up the church and shake it in Satan's face. "This is all I had," Jesus would say, "this bunch of weak, sinful, crazy Christians, and I still kicked your butt!"

Okay, all of this brings up some questions: If what I've said above is true (and it is), why even bother to talk about it? If the battle with Satan has been won, why not move on to other battles? What does all of this have to do with the person who is in a relationship with Christ? And then, following those questions, what in the world does this have to do with the gift of three free sins?

Let me show you.

There is, of course, so much more to be said about Satan. He is a lot of things, but this isn't a book about him. In fact, I even resent the fact that we have to be bothered with him at all, but it really is important to tell the truth about him. Satan is called the "accuser" of Christians, and John said that he "accuses them day and night" (Revelation 12:8–10). Jesus said that Satan is a "liar and the father of lies" (John 8:44), and in Job we see that he is allowed to afflict Christians. Satan annoys, troubles, frightens, and lies; but he never wins.

TURNING GOOD NEWS INTO BAD

The Christian faith is such good news, but so many of us have made it bad. The wonderful news that Christians have unlimited free sins really is good news; but frankly, it can sound skewed, unchristian, and unbiblical.

I've been saying the things I'm writing in this book for a very long time—even longer than some of your lifetimes—and I've come to expect the kind of reaction I get. A lot of people are angry and upset. And I'm often called a "purveyor of cheap grace," antinomian, and a heretic.

I've been all those things at one time or another, so I don't want to be too arrogant about this, but I honestly think that Satan has a plan of deception that might have something to do with your unease about the concept of free sins.

When I first understood that God wasn't angry at his people and felt that God had called me to tell as many people as I could, I thought, *What a great message! Everybody will think I'm wonderful for telling them. They will be so glad I was willing to speak the truth about the real God.* I even said to myself, *Self, you have a gift to give to people, and they will be so pleased that you gave it to them.*

> Satan has a plan of deception that might have something to do with your unease about the concept of free sins.

While I was writing this, Zach Van Dyke, who teaches conferences on grace for teenagers through Key Life, came into my office laughing. He had just heard something that Tony Campolo—my beloved friend, author, and advocate for the poor and the oppressed—said that was really controversial. Zach said, "Your buddy Tony did it again! He really does rile people up."

Not me. All God wanted me to do was tell those who belonged to Christ that God wasn't angry at them and never would be. My message was positive and comforting: "God will never ever say to you, 'That's it. I've had it with you!'" Great message and one that would surely cause people to like me, reward me, and call me "blessed."

Not even close!

I remember my shock when I first discovered that the reaction to the wonderful message I felt God had given me was the equivalent of poking a stick into a hornet's nest. People were not only angry at what I was saying; they were passionately angry.

I remember one question-and-answer session at a conference where I told people that God wasn't angry at them. A man on the front row raised his hand and said loudly, "I don't like this at all! I believe God is angry—very angry—and I'm glad he is. I know me, and the main thing that keeps me faithful is his holiness and his requirement that I be holy or pay the consequences. When I am not holy, he is angry. That's what God does, and it's how he keeps me in line."

I don't remember at all what I said in response, but it was probably something pastoral like, "Sir, you're a fruitcake and something is bent about you. You like God's anger directed at you? Are you crazy? That's from the pit of hell and it smells like smoke!"

It really did smell like smoke! Do you know why? Because his comment reflected the main business of Satan as he does traffic with God's people. He accuses, condemns, and lies. And it's killing us.

If I were Satan and knew that I couldn't destroy God's people (because the sovereign God wouldn't allow me to touch his own) but I still hated them and God's ways and God's truth, do you know what I would do? I would lie, spin the truth, and defang the gospel in every way possible. I would accuse, condemn, and divide. In short, if my doom really was sure, I would cause as much damage as I possibly could before my career ended in a blaze, sizzling in the "lake of fire" (Revelation 19:20).

Someone has said that Satan will use 99 percent of the truth to float one lie. That's true. In fact, I would suggest that Satan takes truth, twists it, and creates a lie to confuse and confound believers—all with the singular purpose of rendering impotent the most explosive and powerful message the world has ever known.

Now I'm not suggesting that the only reason Christians believe lies about God is because the devil made us believe them. Good heavens! There are plenty of other reasons. Someone has said that one shouldn't attribute to cunning what can be adequately explained by stupidity. Christians are not stupid by and large, but we are a weird bunch with all kinds of issues. Sometimes we believe anything people tell us, especially if they have Doctor, Professor, or Reverend before their names. Some of us aren't the most rational people on the face of the earth, and some of us are way too rational. Some of us read too few books, and some of us read too many. When you add to that the human proclivity to believe a lot of unbelievable stuff, there are lots of reasons we believe things that aren't true.

But when the clear teaching of the Bible says one thing and we believe just the opposite, we can be fairly certain that Satan has something to do with it.

You think?

FOUR LIES THAT SMELL LIKE SMOKE

Let me show you how the devil, the father of lies, works. There are four lies (with some truth in them—remember that Satan will use 99 percent of the truth to float one lie) that come from the pit of hell and smell like smoke.

1. Caution

The first lie that comes from the pit of hell and smells like smoke is caution.

There is no question that the Bible warns and admonishes believers to be careful about some things. In fact, the laws of God weren't given to keep us from doing nasty things. The law, among other things, tells Christians where the minefields are in life. God, who loves us, shows us the way we should walk if we want to keep from getting blown up. The law, properly understood, is one of the most wonderful and precious gifts God has given his people.

When I speak, I often say that I like to give some take-away value to those who are listening but aren't Christians: if you want to be happier and better off than you are, find out what the Bible says and live by it as much as you can. "I personally don't care," I will often say, "if you believe in God or think the Bible is true. I'm not your mother. But if you do what I tell you, you'll rise up and call me 'blessed' for having told you." How could I say something like that? The Bible tells us the way things work, and the law of God tells us the places where we need to be careful so we don't get hurt.

But with all of that said, our Christian caution is killing us. If I hear one more time that we have to be careful with this "grace thing" because people will take advantage of it, I'm going to use some very unclergylike language. That's like telling a baby we have to be careful about food or he or she will take advantage of it; refusing to tell an heir about a million-dollar inheritance because we're afraid he or she will take advantage of it; or being careful about education because students will take advantage of it.

I recently saw a bumper sticker that read, "God loves you! But don't let it go to your head!" What's with that? Of course you should let it go to your head. If God loves you and it doesn't go to your head, you just haven't understood. If the God of the universe really likes you, that ought to put everything else into perspective. It should make you laugh and dance with great joy. It might even cause those who don't understand to say about you what they said about the apostles (see Acts 2:13)—that you are plastered.

> If the God of the universe really likes you, that ought to put everything else into perspective.

If you're forgiven all your sins—past, present, and future—(and if you're a Christian, that's exactly what has happened), if you're going to live forever (and you are), and if you've discovered that the meaning of life isn't what you do but who you are (a beloved child of God), how are you going to take advantage of it? Maybe sin? Maybe say the wrong thing? Maybe be inappropriate?

So?

You were already sinning, you have probably on several occasions said the wrong thing, and who hasn't done inappropriate stuff before? Are we supposed to come to Christ and then become zombies or automatons where God pulls the strings? Of course not. When you come to Christ and know that you're forgiven, the first thing you ought to experience is a freedom that you've never known before. It's the freedom of being accepted exactly where you are without any requirement except your coming to him.

If I were the devil, I would try to keep you from ever seeing that.

You think?

2. Condemnation

The second lie that comes from the pit of hell and smells like smoke is condemnation.

The truth is that there is every reason for us to be condemned. Listen: you don't want justice from God; you want mercy. Why is that? If there were a correlation between our sin and our punishment (i.e., justice), we would have been destroyed a long time ago. "If I were God, I would kick the world to pieces," someone has said. "Aren't you glad that I'm not God?"

The truth is that the Bible doesn't give us grounds for a lot of hope because of our goodness. It says radical and negative things about our hearts, our motivations, and our actions. Paul said that no human being will be "justified" in the eyes of God by his or her goodness (Romans 3:20). In fact, if we only got justice from God, we wouldn't have a prayer.

That's a fact and true. Satan doesn't want you to hear, believe, and live in the other side of the truth: "There is therefore now no condemnation for those who are in Christ Jesus" (Romans 8:1).

One of my favorite devotional books is *The Valley of Vision: A Collection of Puritan Prayers and Devotions.* Let me share a prayer I just read:

I have destroyed myself,
my nature is defiled,

the powers of my soul are degraded;
I am vile, miserable, strengthless . . .

Satan loves those words. They are true words and re-flect the existential reality of who I am. He would have me focus on those words, think about them, and then live my life in the awareness that I'm in serious trouble and condemned. Not only that—in my condemnation, I have this great hope that in my trying to do better, maybe God will notice and be pleased with my efforts. That's the place where most Christians live. We really are trying harder to be better, and even if it isn't working so well, we ought to get some credit for the effort. Or at least we hope we will.

Old Slew Foot will do anything to keep us from read-ing the rest of that prayer, understanding the whole truth of Scripture, and then understanding and applying the message of the good news. Listen to more of that Puritan prayer (the Puritans "got it"):

but my hope is in thee.
If ever I am saved it will be by goodness
undeserved and astonishing,
not by mercy alone but by abundant mercy,
not by grace but by exceeding riches of grace;
And such thou has revealed, promised, exemplified
in thoughts of peace, not of evil.[2]

If I were Satan, I would keep you from all that truth. You think?

3. Control

The third lie that comes from the pit of hell and smells like smoke is control.

Control yourself! How often have you heard that? Sometimes it's couched in the very spiritual words of sermons, sometimes it's taught in books, and sometimes it's spoken by *mature* Christians to the new ones so they won't bring shame on Christ. They are told, "After all that Jesus has done for you, you should . . ." (You can make your own list of what "real" Christians do and don't do.)

Peter wrote that we are to live out our freedom but not to use it as "a cover-up for evil" (1 Peter 2:16). That is true, it makes sense . . . and that's the place where Satan wants you to stop reading. He would have you ignore what Paul said in Galatians 5:1, "For freedom Christ has set us free; stand firm therefore, and do not submit again to a yoke of slavery."

Let me tell you a secret: real, authentic pastors worry about their people and their people's walk with Christ. Wolves in sheep's clothing (or maybe shepherds' clothing) worry too. They worry about their power and control (to say nothing of the money), and as long as they use guilt and manipulation to control you, they keep their power and collect their money. Satan laughs and loves the manipulators.

There is another facet to the lie of control. It is the spurious belief that we are responsible for everybody else, that we're called to be the world's mother (and if not the mother of the whole world, certainly the mother of God's people), and that we are not just our own. Is there some truth to that? Of course there is. We are connected and, as such, must look out for one another and be kind. I should taste the salt of your tears and you should taste mine. We should care that our brothers and sisters walk with Christ, and if you're a Christian leader, God didn't call you to form a committee.

But it is very easy to move from the truth of connection to the lie of responsibility; from the truth of caring to the lie of controlling; and from the truth of love to the lie of smothering.

Satan loves it!

You think?

4. Candor

The final lie that comes from the pit of hell and smells like smoke is candor.

This is the lie where we honestly believe our calling in the world is to "maintain our witness." In other words, if we should slip up, the name of Christ would be shamed. Yes, we really are here to share the good news with the world, and that's the truth. Jesus told us that we are to go into the world to make disciples, but that truth is sometimes perverted to become a lie suggesting that we go into the world and lie about the "product" we're selling. There is no room for telling the truth about who we really are.

The "lie from the lie" is that people will miss Christ if they don't see our goodness, our purity, our obedience, and our faithfulness. So we must always be careful to be good, pure, obedient, and faithful. We can't ever let our true selves show—no room for candor. The serious problem we have is that we simply can't pull it off. That means there will be people who will miss Christ because of us. So, what are we going to do?

Fake it.

That's pretty harsh, and it certainly doesn't start that way. It starts with hiding the bad parts and emphasizing the good parts. For instance, if people tell us that they

> *We hide the pain and the tears, so they think that the Christian faith is only for people who don't bleed, never cry, and who always have silly grins on their faces.*

want the joy we have found in Christ, we make sure that every time we're around those folks, we smile, laugh, and let them see the joy. We hide the pain and the tears, so they think that the Christian faith is only for people who don't bleed, never cry, and who always walk around with silly grins on their faces.

Every so often some sociologist comes up with a study showing that Christians have about as many problems as non-Christians. The study shows that our divorce rate, emotional issues, and dark times are about the same as those of unbelievers. Every time one of those studies comes out, Christians "man the ramparts," trying to show how the studies and the statistics were skewed.

They aren't. The candid truth is, given that the Christian faith is a club where the requirement is to be unqualified, our situation may be even worse than that of unbelievers. If that's true, then why don't we tell everybody? I'll tell you why. It is because we will "hurt our witness," when in fact, just the opposite will happen. Our witness to the world is kind of like the bumper sticker that reads, "Christians aren't perfect, just forgiven." Christians really aren't perfect, together, faithful, and wonderful people . . . but we are loved. That's the truth and the gospel. Are we getting better? Probably, but sometimes (as we've seen) the process is so slow that it's hard to notice. But we are loved, forgiven, and accepted. It's his goodness, not ours. Satan wants to maintain the lie that we'll kill off the Christian message if we say so.

The next time you start focusing on your sin and think there is no way God could love someone like you; the next time you wonder if God will accept you after what you've done and after the great number of times you've done it and gone to him and apologized for having done it; the next time you think that there's a limit to God's love and that that limit has been reached; the next time you

> *The next time you wonder if God will accept you after what you've done . . . remember the lies.*

think that there is no way God will keep on forgiving you and showing mercy . . . remember the lies. Could be that they all come from the pit of hell and smell like smoke.

I once had dinner with Michael Greene—a wonderful British theologian, priest, Christian apologist, and author of a pile of books. Among other places where Michael has served, he was the rector of St. Aldate's Church in Oxford, England. While he was rector there, he made several efforts to reach out to the students and faculty at Oxford. On one occasion, St. Aldate's sponsored a wine-and-cheese-tasting party for the theological faculty at Oxford. (They do church different there!)

At any rate, as the evening wore on, one of the women on the theological faculty got a bit tipsy and leaned over and said to Michael, "You know, don't you, that I don't think that any of this is true?"

Michael told me that he whispered to her, "I know, but don't you wish it were?"

Michael said that she was deeply moved and looked so very sad.

If you're not a believer and you're reading this book, don't you wish that all this were true? And if you're a believer and simply can't accept that the gospel is this good because it's supposed to make you miserable and religious, don't you, too, wish it were true?

Could be that the reason you don't think it's true has to do with the "accuser of the brethren."

You think?

What then? Only that in every way,

whether in pretense or in truth,

Christ is proclaimed, and in that I rejoice.

Yes, and I will rejoice.

—Philippians 1:18

A new commandment I give to you,

that you love one another: just as I have loved you,

you also are to love one another.

By this all people will know that you are my disciples,

if you have love for one another.

—John 13:34–35

10

• • •

A Party Down at the Church

If you're not a believer, you don't have to go to church meetings. If it weren't for some other important stuff, it would be reason enough for you to stay where you are. If I get to heaven and God appoints a moderator and starts to call a meeting, I'll know I'm in hell. (I suppose meetings are necessary, but I'm not sure.)

Not too long ago, some of the young guys in the denomination of which I'm a part got tired of ecclesiastical meetings—"the noise of solemn assemblies"—and decided to do something about it. They accomplished a sort of palace coup and took over our church assembly (it's called a presbytery for those of you who care). For the first time in my life, I look forward to the meetings of our presbytery. Let me tell you why.

I remember the first meeting under the new regime. My young friend (the new moderator) stood before the assembled divines and said, "Things are going to be different here. We need each other, but we spend all our time on business instead of holding up each other's arms and binding up each other's wounds. Today is different, and we are going to start by confessing our sins to each other."

I remember thinking, *Oh sure, when cows fly!*

Then to my shock, the moderator confessed his sins to us, and they weren't popcorn sins either. And he confessed sins where the statute of limitations hadn't run out. When he finished, the silence was . . . well . . . very silent. Our brother had just, as it were, undressed before us, and something supernatural and powerful had happened.

In the silence he said, "Now it's your turn."

One by one, the guys in our meeting stood up and started confessing their sins. They spoke of the jealousy they felt for other pastors, the anger, the unfaithfulness, the inordinate thoughts and deeds, the lack of faith . . . and it went on and on.

I was sitting in the back of the church in my regular place—the grumpy, old white guy everybody knew was irritated by just being there—watching and listening. (Someone has said that old people are already irritated about being old and it takes very little to tick them off.) As the confessional proceeded, it became apparent that one man (that would be me) was not participating in the exercise. Not only that, people were beginning to turn around and look at me expectantly.

I often say to students who can be quite condemning of some Christian leaders with whom they disagree that they "haven't lived long enough or sinned big enough" to even have an opinion on the subject. Well, I've lived a long time, and I've sinned big enough. Everybody at that meeting (including a number of former students) knew it and figured that my confession would be the "mother of all confessions."

Finally, when I was the only one left, I stood up and said, "I know that you're waiting for me. Well, it's not going to happen. Okay? I'm not a gossip and I won't share your secrets, but, frankly, you don't seem very safe to me. And it will be a cold day in a very hot place before I confess to you."

Then I stopped, thought about it, and said, "Maybe . . . uh . . . that's my confession."

There aren't very many safe places left in this world. That's why Jesus created the church. Something has gone terribly wrong, and what he went to a lot of trouble to create—a bridge over troubled waters—has somehow become just another storm not unlike the one from which we sought refuge.

DIRTY SECRETS COMING INTO DIVINE LIGHT

Let me say something that is important, controversial, and true: God designed ("allowed," if you prefer) sin so that we could, by seeing it properly, have a safe place.

If you're a Christian, you probably have, as I have, winced at the revelations of the horrible sin of some of our leaders. Every time a Christian leader falls morally, runs a Ponzi scheme on unsuspecting brothers and sisters in Christ, builds a mansion, or buys a Mercedes from the tithe money from Social Security recipients, or creates an empire that begins to crumble, the rest of us want to run away and become Buddhists. Every time the curtain rolls back and we see the hypocrisy, the greed, and the shallowness of the church, we are all embarrassed and are less arrogant about the church against which, Jesus said, "the gates of hell shall not prevail" (Matthew 16:18). It's hard to be triumphalist with that much dirty underwear hanging out in public.

Listen up! Don't waste the dirt! Don't hide the sinners. They're ours. And in the words of the old and often quoted Pogo cartoon, "We have met the enemy and they is us."

Do you think God is doing something in our midst that we've all missed? Everybody who is reading this has se-crets, and if those secrets were publicly revealed, you would flee in embarrassment from friends, neighbors, and fellow church

> *Do you think God is doing something in our midst that we've all missed?*

members. God, for his own reasons, has revealed a few of the dirty secrets of a few of us. But that is only the surface. A mother lode of secrets has already been uncovered; but I fear that, if we don't start getting this thing right, God won't just stop with *them*.

Could it be that God is playing the mother bird who removes the nest from the baby bird who doesn't want to leave and fly? Maybe God is doing what we refuse to do. It's uncomfortable, but it could be the discomfort of a divine surgeon who won't stop cutting until we are well.

As I'm writing this, the headlines everywhere are about the secret documents released by WikiLeaks. Over 250,000 secret government documents have been released to the press and are being published by outlets like (no surprise) the *New York Times*. Doesn't that just "burn your chicken"?! As an American, I believe that those leaks have put lives in danger, encouraged terrorism, and embarrassed our nation in profound ways. I think the people responsible should be prosecuted, convicted, and strung up.

But with that said, I've read some of the revelations. What I've read is, maybe for the first time in diplomatic history, an honest assessment of what some of our leaders really think. Our diplomats are scrambling to do damage control, but frankly I think that their efforts are like trying to put feathers back into a feather pillow . . . one that has been slashed open, feathers flying to the four winds.

Those leaks include "inappropriate remarks" made by Prince Andrew about a foreign country and how the pompous prince shocked Americans by his rude behavior abroad . . . how King Abdullah of Saudi Arabia urged America to attack and destroy Iran . . . and how a manic-depressive Labor government minister in England is a "hound dog" around women and on a number of occasions sexually harassed them. The documents reveal what our leaders really think about some world leaders, to wit, that French president Sarkozy is an "emperor with no clothes," Italian prime minister Berlusconi is a "feckless, vain, and ineffective leader," North Korean dictator Kim Jong-il is a "flabby old" crazy man, and Russian president Medvedev is a "pale, hesitant" guy who plays Robin to Putin's Batman. And that's only the first reports on the leaked documents.

There is something in me so bent that, as much as I'm angry at the folks who are revealing state secrets, I can't stop laughing. Not only that, something in me suggests that our country and our world would be a lot better off if leaders started saying what is true or, if that isn't possible, at least what they really think. We can't remedy problems unless we are honest about what they are.

But that's way above my pay grade. The church isn't above my pay grade, though, or yours. I suggest that damage control is the most dangerous thing Christians can try to do. Especially when the damage has been done by a sovereign and gracious God who is more concerned with our godliness than our reputations.

Do you know what happened in that ecclesiastical meeting after everybody had confessed their sins? You aren't going to believe this, but there were two prominent and clear repercussions.

The first was tears. The second was laughter.

First, the tears

The tears came from the sin. I believe in the gospel of unlimited free sins, but that doesn't mean I'm happy with you or with me. We worship a God who weeps. The Cross, among other things, is a reflection of the tears of a God who loves, who cares, and who wishes for us a life of freedom from the horrible and destructive sin that binds us, makes us dishonest, and causes us to hide. I want to please him more than I want to please anybody else I know. And when I'm involved in something that's not pleasing to him, I have to change . . .

. . . or he must.

He changed!

Well, God doesn't really change the way we change. He is immutable. His change is in our perception, not in his resolution. A friend of mine, upon reading Augustine, told me he had discovered that the love of God secured the Cross of Christ . . . the Cross of Christ did not secure the love of God. Good point, that. And it reflects the "Lamb that was slain from the foundation of the world" outside of time and space, who has always been pleased with his own despite the lack of anything that would cause his pleasure.

But still, I'm not pleased with my sin or my sins. The older I get, the more I grow tired of me and my sin, the greater sorrow I feel in how slowly I'm growing to be like Jesus, and the more I wince at my own sins more than at those of others. There is a sorrow attached to sin. I have a friend who is old, and he told me the other day that death was a "severe mercy" because he didn't know how much longer he could stand himself.

That, of course, is neurotic. Do you know why?

Because the flip side of the sorrow is joy.

Then, the laughter

The other manifestation at the meeting was laughter— the laughter of the redeemed, the loved, the forgiven, and the "terrible meek."

> It's the laughter and the love, dummy! It isn't fake holiness and counterfeit goodness that attracts others to the One who loves us.

What started out as a serious effort to be authentic ended in a party! And it is the party that attracts the world, revolutionizes the "normal," and smells like Jesus. It's the laughter and the love, dummy! It isn't fake holiness and counterfeit goodness that attracts others to the One who loves us.

GREENSBORO GRUB

It's called the Greensboro Grub (it was called the Nashville Grub before it moved to Greensboro). It's a new way of doing church and sometimes even telling others about Jesus. I'm not even sure that I like it, but I was a part of it once, and I can't stop thinking about it.

Let me give you some background. I have some friends I love a lot, Charlie and Ruth Jones, who often travel with me, doing incredibly dramatic illustrations of God's grace. Their ministry is called Peculiar People (taken from 1 Peter 2:9 in the King James Version), and they really are kind of peculiar. (That makes them a good fit with our staff and what we do!)

Anyway, Charlie and Ruth lived in Nashville for a good many years and would often invite people over to their house for dinner. Charlie is a wonderful chef, and their friends loved those dinners. Then what started out as a fairly intimate dinner with friends began to grow, taking on a life of its own. All kinds of strangers started showing up for the Nashville Grub. The evening would sometimes have religious overtones to it; but more often than not, it would end up with poets reading poetry, dramatists performing, and musicians singing and playing, along with a lot of good food and laughter.

A couple of years ago, at the invitation of a pastor in Greensboro, Charlie and Ruth moved there to see if there was a way to connect with outsiders—those who had been turned off by traditional Christianity. Church didn't connect with those folks, and there was the hope that maybe people as weird and as different as Charlie and Ruth could help.

That's when the fire came! No, no, not that kind of fire. It was the fire of God's Spirit—the "Wild Goose" as the Celts called the Holy Spirit. The Holy Spirit is called the Wild Goose because God's Spirit can't be controlled, directed, manipulated, or placed in a box. As Jesus said, it is like the wind that "blows where it wishes" (John 3:8). Charlie and Ruth started walking the streets, listening, accepting, and loving; and then the fire came.

I got a chance to go to Greensboro to "help" Charlie and Ruth. It turned out that the time wasn't for them, but for me. It was a time for me to get warm by their fire. God was trying to help this old cynical preacher become a bit less cynical.

Charlie and Ruth are in the process of buying an old historic hotel in downtown Greensboro. (While it is historic, the word *historic* doesn't really describe what it is. It is, in fact, an old dilapidated building that has seen far better days.) So they invited Nashville recording artist Buddy Greene (he sometimes travels with us, too, and he loves Charlie and Ruth as much as I do) and me to come to Greensboro to help them raise funds to buy the hotel. I talked (that's what I do) and Buddy sang (it's what he does), and we got to experience the Greensboro Grub.

Let me give you a bit of the flavor of the Greensboro Grub from the perspective of a reporter, Tina Firesheets, who is with the Greensboro *News and Record*. The newspaper piece is headlined "Massive dinner is all about connecting." The reporter wrote about the "gathering" for dinner in the old hotel . . . and the love. Charlie and Ruth's pastor, Jim White, said about the dinners, "We think that what they're doing is great for the city . . . inviting people up, loving them, feeding them, sharing their lives together. What can be better than that?"

Dinner with friends consists of nearly 60 guests, 118 shrimp toast rounds, a 25-pound roast beef, a 22-pound country ham, 16 pounds of collard greens, six gallons of red beans and nine pounds of kielbasa sausage. And that's not even the entire menu. . . . It's all home-cooked, and it takes three days to prepare and at least one day to clean up afterward.

After dinner there was music, poetry readings, dramatic sketches, and laughter. Then a sketch about Brad Pitt and Angelina Jolie. Angelina misses Brad and their children, and Brad fantasizes about his ex-wife, Jennifer Aniston. People are laughing.

The reporter continues:

When the quirky performance finally ends, Charlie Jones wonders if they should ban improv (isation): "I never thought I'd say we need to have standards to the Grub."

His skit with Ruth Jones is the last of the evening. Their performance about a grief-stricken woman at a hospital who finds hope where she least expects it—a mentally challenged orderly—draws a few tears.

Charlie Jones may be an actor, but the emotion that comes at the end of each Grub is genuine. His blue eyes fill with tears that he manages to retain. He ends each Grub by thanking them for coming.

And then comes the moment they all wait for. It's a

phrase that has become his trademark, and it signals the end of the evening.

"Now, get the hell out of my house," he says.

Everyone laughs. It's time to go.[1]

I'm sharing this with you because what is going on at the Greensboro Grub is church. It's not all that church is, and I'm certainly not suggesting that when we do church it has to be done that way. I'm a Bach guy, and I'm big on pipe organs and normal church stuff. However, I *am* suggesting that every church ought to smell like the Greensboro Grub. The celebration, the love, the laughter, the freedom, the authenticity—and yes, even the earthiness— should be the mark of church when Jesus is in attendance.

How do we get there? Three free sins! That's how.

INVITING OTHERS TO THE PARTY

But this chapter isn't just about a party; it's about inviting people to the party. Jesus said that when he was "lifted up" (i.e., hung on the cross and then proclaimed), he would "draw all people" to himself (John 12:32).

The last time I checked, that hasn't happened. That either means that Jesus was wrong (probably not) or that there is something wrong with the lifting-up part (probably).

There is an old story about St. Francis visiting a village

where he discovered that a church had been erected and named after him. He directed his monks to tear down the church. As he and his monks walked out of the village, one of the monks said to St. Francis, "I thought we came here to preach?"

"We did!" St. Francis answered.

St. Francis is often credited with the statement that we ought "to preach the gospel always and, when necessary, use words." Whether or not he said it, it was a profound comment about what it means to lift Jesus up.

If you are a part of the church, it is a truism: we are here for "them." In other words, our business is to lift up Christ so that those who need to be loved, forgiven, and accepted might run to him. That is called "evangelism," a word taken from a Greek word meaning "good news." Thus an evangelist is a person who brings good news, and evangelism is the way we bring it.

Doing evangelism is about "them," but the methodology is far more about us than it is about them.

Evangelism—may God have mercy on us (and he does)—has become an enterprise defined by numbers, competition, and technique. Americans are quite good at enterprise. Focus, train, and build! We do that with business, banks, and books. And it is only natural for us to go

> Evangelism—may God have mercy on us (and he does)—has become an enterprise defined by numbers, competition, and technique.

about the "business" of evangelism the same way we go about everything else. There are even evangelistic ministries that solicit funds on the basis of how much "bank for the buck" the giver will get (i.e., how many souls per dollar).

I have a Jewish friend who, after he became a Christian, contacted a number of major and well-known evangelistic ministries posing as a major donor. (He was a new Christian then and didn't know that what he was doing lacked integrity, so he did it anyway.) The statistics were way off. He found out that every citizen of the United States had been "saved" and "saved" several times!

I'm not throwing rocks or even suggesting that God hasn't used our less-than-perfect methodologies. Frankly, I never would have come to the forgiveness and love that I've experienced were it not for some of those skewed methodologies.

I'm talking about my beloved family here. Sometimes we/I meant well and the ways we did evangelism came from hearts that honestly wanted others to know Christ. We wanted to do it the best way, and at the time our methods seemed best . . . but that was when we had money and power. We now have less of both, and God has started advertising our sins to the whole world. Don't you hate it?

DOING EVANGELISM THE WAY JESUS DID IT

Now, we have to do evangelism the way Jesus did it. And I don't believe that we can ever lift up Christ in a way that anybody cares about until and when we understand the amazing gift of God. You guessed it! Three free sins. Let me show you.

1. Jesus showed up.

Scripture says that "the Word became flesh and dwelt among us" (John 1:14).

The word *church* comes from a Greek word (*ekklesia*) meaning to be "called out" or the "called out ones"—we are "called out" of the world. I get that, but the problem is when we are "called out" without being "sent back" into the world to teach others. (Jesus said that just as God had sent him, he was sending us, John 20:21.) We have a tendency to build walls and then invite people to "come join us" behind the safe walls. Someone has described the church service as a bland man standing in front of bland people telling them to become blander. I don't subscribe to that description, but there is enough truth in it to sting.

What's wrong with us? I'll tell you what is true, at least for me. I have a whole lot to protect, a whole lot to hide, and a whole lot to defend. I'm ordained, and it is of utmost existential importance that I do a lot of protecting, hiding, and defending. After all, I need this job.

That's my problem. What's yours?

The truth is that there is no problem if we are a people who have accepted the gift of unlimited free sins. Then we won't have anything to hide or defend. Nobody's reputation needs to be protected! Jesus' reputation is unassailable, and ours is not. I suggested earlier that the very fact that we are Christians (properly understood) is a statement to the world that we are extremely needy, terribly sinful, and really weak. We are a part of a club that requires nothing of its members except that they recognize they are a part of a club that requires nothing from its members. And that's because we can't meet any other requirement.

When Christians get to the point where they read only Christian books, go only to Christian movies, hang out only with other Christians, eat only Christian cookies, and wear only Christian underwear, it's time for a reality check. That's sick, and it is a sickness unto death.

Once we are set free from the need to defend, protect, and hide, we have the freedom to show up in places where proper Christians don't go for fear of getting dirty. And it is in our showing up that the authenticity of who we are becomes the "flavor" that attracts others to the ice-cream maker.

So, go do something that isn't religious. Just show up. It's called evangelism.

2. Jesus identified.

Jesus not only showed up; he identified. There is a truly amazing statement in Hebrews 2:17–18 about Jesus: "Therefore he had to be made like his brothers in every respect, so that he might become a merciful and faithful high priest in the service of God, to make propitiation for the sins of the people. For because he himself has suffered when tempted, he is able to help those who are being tempted."

There is an old story about a Texas church that adhered to the doctrine of baptismal sanctification, which means that after a person is baptized, that person no longer sins. A good ole boy heard the message and wanted to be baptized. The problem was that it was the middle of the winter and the river was frozen over. Nevertheless, he insisted. So the congregation gathered at the river, chiseled out a hole in the ice, and the pastor and one of the deacons went with the new convert down into the cold water. They pushed him under and when he came up, the new convert shouted, "Praise God. I'm free of sin and it's wonderful. I don't even feel the cold!"

"We've got to do it again," the deacon said through chattering teeth. "He's lying."

There is, of course, a difference between Jesus' identification with sin and our own. Jesus identified with it by being tempted; our identification with sin runs much deeper. When Paul called himself the "chief of sinners," he was able to identify with sin all by himself, but because of his identification with Jesus, he found mercy. Paul went on to say, "I received mercy for this reason, that in me, as the foremost [sinner], Jesus Christ might display his perfect patience as an example to those who were to believe in him for eternal life" (1 Timothy 1:16).

> *Paul was able to identify with sin all by himself, but because of his identification with Jesus, he found mercy.*

The good news of the incarnation is that when we run to Jesus with our pain, our failure, and our need, he always says first, "I know, child, I know." When we start saying the same thing to them (those who aren't believers), they may start listening.

It's called evangelism.

3. Jesus loved.

Jesus not only showed up and identified; he loved. John makes a wonderful comment about Jesus just before John begins to describe the events leading up to Jesus' death. He writes, "Now before the Feast of the Passover, when Jesus knew that his hour had come to depart out of this world to the Father, having loved his own who were in the world, he loved them to the end" (John 13:1).

You've got to be kidding! He loved that bunch? They couldn't even stay awake with him when he was in agony; all of them were cowards who ran when the battle needed someone to stand; their leader denied even knowing him. He loved that selfish bunch? Yeah, he did, and I don't understand it either.

Now that I think about it, I don't know how in the world he loves me. But he does—and without condition and with unrelenting determination and unwavering resolve. I often sense his love in my heart, a love informed by Scripture when he says, "I love you. I don't care if you don't love me or if you don't want me around. I still love you. So deal with it." (That's the SBV—the Steve Brown version of Scripture.)

And insofar as I do "deal with it" (allow him to love me by accepting his gift of forgiveness—free sins), something strange happens to my attitude toward *them*. I find myself (despite myself) loving the other sinners, robbers, and scoundrels who need love as much as I do. And when I let it show in places where one doesn't expect a Christian to show up, it's called evangelism.

4. Jesus laughed.

Finally, there is one other thing about Jesus' way of doing evangelism. He not only showed up, identified, and loved; he laughed. I know. Jesus was a man of sorrows, but that was partly because he didn't want us to be "people of sorrow." He said, "These things I have spoken to you, that my joy may be in you, and that your joy may be full" (John 15:11).

Philip Yancey, in an address he gave to Christians in Saudi Arabia, had some profound things to say about how Christians can cope with being a small and persecuted minority. Among his remarks:

Recently I have been reading a historical study by Rodney Stark, *The Rise of Christianity*. A sociologist of religion, Stark investigated the success of the early Christian movement, which, starting from a few thousand followers, grew to encompass half the population of the Roman Empire in three centuries. In the midst of a hostile environment, the Christians simply acted on their beliefs. Going against the majority culture, they treated slaves as human beings, often liberating them, and elevated women to positions of leadership. When an epidemic hit their towns, they stayed behind to nurse the sick. They refused to participate in such common practices as abortion and infanticide. They responded to persecution as martyrs, not as terrorists. And when Roman social networks disintegrated, the church stepped in. Even one of their pagan critics had to acknowledge that early Christians loved their neighbors "as if they were our own family."[2]

Then Philip went on to describe how the Christians shined because they were different, held different values, and lived out those different values before the watching world. Christianity in those days was counter culture. I, of course, agree with that; but it's way too much for me and far too religious. It feels like another call to "be good" so that the world will see the difference. It's a call to be an "example" . . . and I don't do that very well.

But maybe I can be "salt" and "light." Salt is only good for making something else taste better, and light is, in my case, always a reflection of an outside source that shines in the darkness. I can, I think, stay close to him and, insofar as I can, get out of the way. Christians in the first century lived out who they were.

I can do that. I'm tired of pretending anyway.

And you know what? I find myself laughing a lot. Every time I remember that I'm forgiven and loved (that I have unlimited free sins and blank checks), I get the giggles. In fact, Christians are the only people on earth who have something significant to laugh about. And when the world comes to our party, hears our laughter, and joins us in our dancing . . .

. . . it's called evangelism.

Have no fear of them,

for nothing is covered that will not be revealed,

or hidden that will not be known.

What I tell you in the dark, say in the light,

and what you hear whispered, proclaim on the housetops.

—Matthew 10:26–27

Even if we or an angel from heaven

should preach to you a gospel contrary to

the one we preached to you, let him be accursed.

—Galatians 1:8

11
• • •
Just Don't Let Them!

If you're not religious and can't buy into this Jesus thing, you might want to skip this chapter. I'm going to talk to those who are a part of my faith family, the family I love a lot. There are some family matters we have to attend to in this chapter, and you don't have to be present if you don't want to be.

My friend Norm Evans, former Miami Dolphins and Seattle Seahawks football player and the founder of Pro Athletes Outreach, told me once about a college football lineman who was in his first college football game. During a time-out he said to the coach, "Their lineman keeps pulling my helmet down over my eyes. What should I do?"

"Son," the coach said quietly, "Don't let him."

I've often thought that Christian publishers should have a rule that any author of a book dealing with what's wrong with the church and Christians should, by publishing law, be required to devote the first chapter of his or her book to a confession of his or her own sins. It's hard to listen to people who "speak from Sinai," whose familiarity with sin seems to be hearsay, whose ecclesiastical robes are white, and whose fingernails are clean.

I think I've confessed enough of my own failure and sin in this book to say something that needs to be said. And not only that, at the very beginning of this chapter, you should know that I'm talking about "us" and not just "them" or "you." Frankly, I'm about as guilty of what follows as anybody I know. What we have done to one another is unconscionable! In fact, it may be the moral equivalent of a suicide pact.

WOLVES AMONG US

Jesus said, "Beware of false prophets, who come to you in sheep's clothing but inwardly are ravenous wolves" (Matthew 7:15). There are wolves in our midst. They are not the unbelievers who hate the church or the sinners whose disobedience hurts the reputation of the church. Those wolves aren't the heretics either or those who get their theology wrong. All of those people can create problems, but the wolves I'm talking about are those who have the reputation of godliness and, unfortunately, have believed their own PR. That alone is bad enough, but they don't stop there. They fleece the lambs of God (that would be us), looking down their long spiritual noses with their peacock feathers flying in the breeze and saying things like, "After all that Jesus has done for you, one would think you would [you can fill in the blank]. You bring shame on the name of Christ. Jesus said that our works should indicate who we are, but your works for him leave *much* to be desired. Have you considered that you may not be saved?"

Then if you are "building an empire for Jesus," you take up a collection.

In the book of Acts, when Paul was on his way to Rome, where he would face some major trials and a good possibility that he would be executed, he asked the leaders of his beloved church in Ephesus to meet him on the dock at the harbor in Miletus. Everybody was aware that this could very well be the last time they would meet together, and there were lots of tears. Paul said to those leaders, "Pay careful attention to yourselves and to all the flock, in which the Holy Spirit has made you overseers, to care for the church of God, which he obtained with his own blood. I know that after my departure fierce wolves will come in among you, not sparing the flock; and from among your own selves will arise men speaking twisted things, to draw away the disciples after them. Therefore be alert" (Acts 20:28–31).

Who were the "fierce wolves" Paul spoke about? They're not who you think they are. We're going to talk about that in a moment, but first I want to give you a quote from Bill Hendricks. A number of years ago, Bill

Hendricks decided to go to the back doors of churches and find out why people were leaving. (Most "seeker driven" studies asked why they came and helped churches design their services around what they discovered.) He published his findings in a book titled *Exit Interviews*.

Hendricks came up with a number of conclusions, and among them was the fact that a lot of Christians speak the "language" of grace but the reality of grace is missing. Let me share his words:

> And therein lies a crisis, especially for the conservative side of the church. Based on the stories present here, I believe that the church needs to decide how long it is going to coddle legalism in its ranks. By legalism I mean people who preach grace but practice works. People who inflict guilt on others for being human, let alone sinful. People who say, "Well, we don't want to go overboard on this grace thing because people will take advantage of it."
>
> The church has made it comfortable for those who hold that position. But at what cost? It is keeping people out of the church, it is driving people away from the church, and it is poisoning the lives of those who remain in the church.
>
> So why permit it? Why even tolerate it, especially when Jesus and Paul, among others, reserved their harshest words for those who compromised grace.[1]

WHO ARE THE WOLVES?

Okay, let's talk about wolves.

When we read Paul's words to those leaders from Ephesus and listen to his warning about the wolves, we have to be careful not to read what he said in our own cultural context and through the lens of our biases. Depending on who we are and what we do, wolves take on all kinds of personae. For Reformed people, it's those who aren't Reformed. For Pentecostal folks, it can be those cold, dead Christians who haven't been baptized in the Spirit. For Anglicans and Catholics, it could be those cretins who don't understand the importance of the liturgy and the power of the sacraments. For the legalists, it's the people who are using their liberty as license. For liberals, it's conservatives; for conservatives, it's liberals. Those who are orthodox are sure that the wolves are the heretics, and the less orthodox are sure that fundamentalists are the wolves. For those of us who are traditional, it's the television preachers offering shallow pap for thousands of the unwary; and for them, it's the uptight theological types who are more interested in propositions than people. Most of us think that the wolves are people who have compromised the theological and moral standards that have always been a part of the "faith that was once for all delivered to the saints" (Jude 1:3).

As a matter of fact, that's not the wolves about whom

Paul is speaking at all. *Who are the wolves?* If you want to know, all you have to do is flip over to the book of Galatians, where Paul is dealing with wolves. Paul's fear for his beloved friends at Ephesus was a fear grounded in hard experience. He had been there, done that, and had a closetful of bloodied, wolf-torn T-shirts. Paul didn't like sin or bad theology, he hated divisions, and he was worried about all kinds of institutional problems . . . but the wolves were different and far scarier. The wolves were those who would pervert the gospel. And at the same time, they were (and are) often those who seem to be the most obedient, the most godly, and the most spiritual.

> *The wolves were those who would pervert the gospel.*

The book of Galatians is often called the Magna Carta of Christian Liberty. Its writing was occasioned by the coming of some very religious, very uptight, and very wrong believers who were scandalized with the message of the gospel.

Paul was shocked, and we should be too. He wrote, "I am astonished that you are so quickly deserting him who called you in the grace of Christ and are turning to a different gospel" (Galatians 1:6). Paul was earthy in his opposition to the wolves, and we should be too. He said, "I wish those who unsettle you would emasculate themselves!" (Galatians 5:12). (Now that's strong!) Paul spared no one in his defense of the gospel, and we shouldn't either. He even pointed out that Peter was a hypocrite in these matters (see Galatians 2:13). Paul refused to join hands and sing "Kumbaya" around the campfire with those who compromised the gospel of grace. And we should avoid that too. Paul said, "Even if we or an angel from heaven should preach to you a gospel contrary to the one we preached to you, let him be accursed" (Galatians 1:8).

Martin Luther reflects Paul's anger in his irritation with the wolves. He wrote:

> I believe that it has now become clear that it is not enough or in any sense "Christian" to preach the works, life, and words of Christ . . . as if the knowledge of these would suffice for the conduct of life. . . . Yet, this is the fashion among those who today [1500s] are regarded as our best preachers . . . and such teaching is childish and effeminate nonsense.
>
> Rather ought Christ to be preached to the end that faith in Him may be established that He may not only be Christ, but be Christ for you and me, and that which is said of Him and is denoted in His name may be effectual in us. Such faith is produced and preserved in us by preaching why Christ came, what He brought and bestowed, what benefit it is to us to accept Him . . . What person is there whose heart, upon hearing these things, will not rejoice to its depth and when receiving such comfort will not grow tender so that they will love

Christ as they never could by means of any law or work?

There are some who have no understanding to hear the truth of freedom and insist upon their goodness as means for salvation. These people you must resist, do the very opposite, and offend them boldly lest by their impious views they drag many with them into error. For the sake of liberty of the faith do other things which they regarded as the greatest of sins . . . use your freedom constantly and consistently in the sight of and despite the tyrants and stubborn so that they may learn that they are impious, that their law and works are of no avail for righteousness, and that they had no right to set them up.[2]

WOLFOLOGY 101

Now let's study Wolfology 101 and look at its destructive power. The basic textbook for the course is Galatians, with ancillary readings in a number of other biblical sources. There are four basic truths about wolves that you ought to know.

When you see any of these things happening, run.

No, don't run. *Fight.* Paul said that we should "stand firm" and not "submit" (Galatians 5:1).

1. Wolves distort the good news.

First, you should be aware of the MO of the wolves— their disguised, subtle, and manipulative pressure. Paul said that they worked to "distort" the good news of Christ (Galatians 1:7) and that they even manipulated Peter and Barnabas into sharing their hypocrisy (see Galatians 2:11–14). Paul wrote, "Yet because of false brothers secretly brought in—who slipped in to spy out our freedom that we have in Christ Jesus, so that they might bring us into slavery—to them we did not yield in submission even for a moment, so that the truth of the gospel might be preserved for you" (Galatians 2:4–5).

Do you remember the friend "J" I told you about in chapter one, the one who has HIV? Nobody knows that except me, his physician, and God. My friend gave me permission to tell you about him, and he asked me to ask you to pray for him as God brings him to mind. He walks a very hard road. I'm not sure how I learned his story, but I suppose "J" gave me bits of his soul early on to see if I could be trusted and then let me know the whole truth. It isn't pretty. He continues to struggle with same-sex attraction and now HIV, but the real struggle isn't with his sin (we all live in that house) but with other Christians.

My friend grew up in a church where there were "strong standards." The leaders constantly taught and imposed those standards, even forbidding their members to read C. S. Lewis's Space Trilogy because of its occult content. If you were to attend that church, you would be amazed at their commitment, their refusal to compromise, and their stand for truth. You would commend their efforts to keep the purity of the church intact and their

Scripture-memorization program. They will love you—and they talk a lot about love—but only if you agree with their doctrine and conform to their standards.

My friend realized early on that he was "different" and told me that he often wept before God, begging God to remove the horrible sinful desires from his heart and to "keep him pure." Then he fell, and in the falling became HIV positive.

Let me quote "J":

I know you say you love the church, Steve, and I say this in love, but you can have her. She is not my bride. My experience with this whore has left me a twisted-up, broken man and I hate her for it. Her self-righteousness, her arrogance, her lack of compassion, and her willingness to allow the lost to fall head first into hell, reminds me more of Babylon than of Christ. She has left me confused and bewildered. I don't know who God is. I don't know whether to run to God for help or go ahead and blow myself away in despair.

Who are you, God? Are you like the church I've known? Are you like those who condemn anyone that offers the world a shred of hope, or a small cup of compassion? Do you trample the weak under your feet? Do you crush the sinner like the grapes in the winepress?

You know the amazing thing about my friend? He is still running to Jesus . . . and not the one the wolves lied about. "J" sent me a prayer letter he wrote to God. I wept when I read it:

> *Dear God,*
>
> *I'm sorry for my behavior lately. I'm sorry that I don't go to church, or read your word, or do the stuff I once did to get You to like me. I'm sorry that I'm not the best witness to the world around me. I'm usually stressed-out, worried, afraid, and so shy that I don't talk much to anyone about You. I hope You can forgive me. I'm also sorry that I sometimes get mad at You.*
>
> *Do You still love me? Do You still want me around? Do You still love me as much as I want to love You?*
>
> *I feel so lost and alone.*
>
> *But God, I submit my spirit to You . . . and will wait. Please don't let my suffering and pain harden my heart or destroy my faith in Your love.*

As I told you, I wept when I read his prayer, but I was irritated too. If my friend's sin irritates you more than those who robbed him of God's grace, then I'm irritated at you too!

> *"I'm stressed-out, worried, afraid, and so shy that I don't talk much to anyone about You. I hope You can forgive me."*

Don't let them do that to you!

2. Wolves have hidden agendas.

There is more that you need to know about wolves. You must also be constantly aware of the hidden agendas of wolves. Paul wrote, "They make much of you, but for no good purpose. They want to shut you out, that you may make much of them" (Galatians 4:17).

There is money in religion! And if you do it right, you can get power and prestige too. I have a friend who says that if you make your living at religion, you are going to lose one or the other. While I'm not sure I agree with that entirely—I am, after all, writing this book with the hope that you will buy it and thus enable me to make the mortgage and put food on the table—my friend has pointed to a great danger—the danger of hidden agendas.

I have a couple of doctorates, but they're phony. While I work with professors who have their PhDs from such places as Harvard, Cambridge, Duke, and Oxford, mine were given to me for speaking at graduations at academic institutions. Not only did they make me a "doctor" when I'm not even a nurse, they paid me for giving the speeches. It doesn't get much better than that! I thought, as did the farmer who found oil on his back forty, "Now they'll listen to me."

That often happens with ordination too. Before, we taught Sunday school and maybe even served in the leadership of a local congregation, but now we're different, and they listen because we're ordained. Now don't get me wrong. If we're saying something biblical, true, and helpful, it's good that people listen. The problem happens when we find that we can parlay their listening into power, prestige, and money. It is a short trip from being told that one is very close to God to the feeling that one speaks from Sinai. Empires have been built on far less.

When the wolves start laying burdens on the sheep, it's always wise for the sheep to ask: "What's in it for him or her? Where is the payback? Am I funding a leader's dream, or God's dream? Do I worship at a guru's altar, or at God's? Am I being set free, or put under a burden of guilt and condemnation in order to make him or her feel better?"

Don't let them do that to you!

3. Wolves impose heavy burdens on sheep.

And speaking of burdens, that brings me to the third truth about wolves. Wolves impose heavy burdens on the sheep. Paul described what was happening in Galatia as an effort on the part of the wolves to impose a "yoke of slavery" on the sheep (Galatians 5:1). Slaves are not free; their job is to maintain the freedom and the power of the slave owners.

That bothered Jesus too. Matthew 23 is enough to make any leader of God's people wince. Every time I read that chapter, it scares the spit out of me—"hypocrites," "whitewashed tombs," "blind," "killers" of prophets. And the thing that's scary about Jesus' words is that they were addressed to the most religious, most committed, and most godly people around. If you're a leader of other Christians and that doesn't scare you, you're dead.

But for our purpose here, listen to one of the things

Jesus said: "They tie up heavy burdens, hard to bear, and lay them on people's shoulders, but they themselves are not willing to move them with their finger" (v. 4). You can determine the "wolfness" of a Christian wolf by noticing how guilty, tired, and condemned you feel in his or her presence.

> *You can determine the "wolfness" of a Christian wolf by noticing how guilty, tired, and condemned you feel in his or her presence.*

Religion will make you weird. Do you know why? Because God is such a central part of our DNA. It's everywhere. My friend Terry Mattingly, who writes a nationally syndicated column ("On Religion") for the Scripps Howard News Service, is also the editor of a wonderful website, Get Religion (www.getreligion.org), based on the premise that the "press doesn't get religion." In fact he suggests that the press often doesn't even recognize that it's there.

Terry writes about the ghosts that are a part of journalism:

> One minute they are there. The next they are gone. There are ghosts in there, hiding in the ink and the pixels. Something is missing in the basic facts, or perhaps most of the key facts are there, yet some are twisted. Perhaps there are sins of omission, rather than commission. A lot of these ghosts are, well, holy ghosts. They are facts and stories and faces linked to

the power of religious faith. Now you see them. Now you don't. In fact, a whole lot of the time you don't get to see them. But that doesn't mean they aren't there.[3]

Everything is about God (we were created that way—what we think, how we feel about ourselves and others, how we act, the friends we have, the places we go, how we sleep and with whom we sleep, our value, and our meaning). Even the new atheists who are so hot and bothered about God are about God. Ever wonder why people who don't believe in Santa Claus or the Easter Bunny don't feel the need to write whole books about why they don't exist? Because Santa Claus and the Easter Bunny are not part of who we are.

Just so, if God weren't a part of their DNA, the new atheists would not write such sophomoric drivel. It's about God. It's who we are, and we can't help it.

Now, assuming you buy into what I just said, this God thing in us is not altogether different from hunger, sexual desire, or the drive for peace and security; only it's far bigger. If hunger can make you fat, sexual desire cause you to turn others into objects instead of people, and the desire for peace and security cause you to take peace and security from others, think what the desire for God will do. If we distort our lesser passions, how much more our passion for God?

The wolves know that! Someone has said that we southerners get away with saying anything, no matter how hurtful or critical, by prefacing what we say with "Bless your heart . . ." Well, Christians can lay on the guilt, rob the sheep of their freedom, send them on a crusade to impact the world, and "turn the tide for God," all with a prophetic "Thus says the Lord." That's why, when new Christians come into the church, we put saddles on them and ride them until they die. And the great tragedy is that our neurotic DNA makes us think we're doing it for him.

Don't let them do that to you!

4. Wolves lie about God.

Finally, be careful to note the God the wolves would have you worship. They lie about God and sometimes even for what are laudable reasons. Their God becomes a monster and a child abuser. They preach about his wrath and his jealousy. They tell you he will take away your salvation if you tell a lie (or pick your sin of choice) and don't repent of it before you die. They will make God into a celestial policeman who is looking for ways to catch you doing something wrong or something that displeases him, and if he does, will break your legs. And the wolves will go absolutely ballistic when someone suggests that you have free sins.

Paul was having none of it. In fact, he countered the lies with the truth. He said that he had been crucified with Christ (not a command but a fact for every believer) "and the life I now live in the flesh I live by faith in the Son of God, who loved me and gave himself for me" (Galatians 2:20). "But when the fullness of time had come, God sent forth his Son, born of woman, born under the law, to redeem those who were under the law, so that we might receive adoption as sons. And because you are sons, God has sent the Spirit of his Son into our hearts, crying, 'Abba! ["daddy" or "papa"!] Father!' So you are no longer a slave, but a son, and if a son, then an heir through God" (Galatians 4:4–7).

They will make you feel like an orphan! The wolves will say that God's patience is such that, if you continue in your sin, he will say, "That's it! I've had it with you." God never says that!

Don't let them do that to you!

If you're still with me, you know the truth that no profound relationship can be established with God until you come to him with nothing to offer but your sin. You also know that the relationship with him is not maintained by your obedience and righteousness but by his grace and Christ's righteousness. You know, too, that power comes from living an ongoing life of repentance (knowing who you are, who God is, what you've done, and then "putting the ball in God's court" by telling him). Further, you know that until we recognize and proclaim that to our brothers and sisters in Christ and to those who aren't a part of our family, we will remain in the concrete of our self-righteousness and the hardness of our prison cells.

Anybody who tells you differently is a wolf.

Oh, and one other thing before I finish.

I recently came across a statement made by Jonathan Edwards that gave me pause and especially so after what I've written in this chapter. "Some people," he wrote, "are full of talk against legal doctrines, legal preaching and the legal spirit. Yet they may understand very little of what they are talking against. A legal spirit is far more subtle than they imagine. It can lurk, operate, and prevail in their hearts even while they are inveighing against it."[4]

While I don't think so, I suppose I could be doing what Jonathan Edwards warned against.

If so, I repent!

Now it's your turn!

We know in part . . .

—1 Corinthians 13:9

Go, inquire of the LORD for me,

and for the people, and for all Judah,

concerning the words of this book that has been found.

—2 Kings 22:13

12
• • •
Are You Crazy?

At the ministry where I serve, Key Life Network, we get thousands of questions and spend a considerable amount of time and effort on our broadcasts, on our websites, in our publications, and in emails and letters, answering those questions. Before we begin with the questions posed, let me say to you what I often say in answering questions.

I am often wrong!

I'm not your mother!

I take you and your questions seriously.

I've written and spoken on the subjects addressed in this book for a whole lot of years. What follows are actual questions that I've often been asked regarding the subject of freedom and grace.

1. Are you crazy?

Sometimes I think so. In fact, the things we Christians say we believe are quite crazy. We believe that there is a God who created everything, and who especially and lovingly created us. We believe that creator God is in charge of all that creation and directs it for his purposes. Then we believe that the same God humbled himself and became a man, walking our dirty roads, hanging out with the worst of us, and then hanging on a cross for his people. We believe that that dead man got out of a grave and walked around, was taken up to heaven, and will return to clean up the mess.

If you believe that, you'll believe anything!

But if that doesn't cause you to wince, this will: The Bible teaches that God likes us a lot. And that our sin isn't the issue, and it was covered on the cross. Not only that, we believe that the goodness of Christ himself was given to us and that we stand good before God because of that gift.

Paul called the gospel the "foolishness of God" (1 Corinthians 1:25) and said it "pleased God through the folly of what we preach to save those who believe" (v. 21).

There is a sense in which what seems logical, balanced, and reasonable probably isn't the gospel; but rather, it's people trying to create a God they think ought to exist. That's called "religion," and it's easy to win arguments with that religion. The truth of the gospel is so *foolish* that you have to *get* it rather than understand it. If you don't *get* it, those who do seem crazy.

*2. Why do you persist in irritating everybody? Free sins?
That's outrageous! Why don't you write and teach in
a normal way?*

I've tried to say it in a *normal* way. Nobody listens. So I
decided to ditch the theological and religious words, and
to be as outrageous as God was in his giving of himself for
us. It sometimes makes people angry, but they do listen.

*3. There are a lot of examples in the Bible that show God's
wrath, and yet you say that God isn't angry at his people.
Are you sure you haven't gotten it wrong?*

Hermeneutics helps.

4. What's hermeneutics?

Hermeneutics is the science of interpretation (I
looked it up). In order to understand what God is doing
in the world and in our lives, it is important that we understand the way God revealed himself.

He started out with some really bad news about his
wrath and our sin. And he used Israel (in the Old Testament) to demonstrate the bad news and the good news:
The bad news was that when you are disobedient, God will
"break your face." The good news was that if you do it
right, good things will happen to you. Much of the Bible
is a true revelation of the holiness of God and teaches that
it is a "fearful thing to fall into the hands of the living
God" (Hebrews 10:31). So God used Israel and the Old
Testament to teach the bad news. (Some of my Jewish

friends tell me that they sometimes wish God had chosen the Italians.)

It's hard to hear good news until you first know the bad news—and God used Israel and the Old Testament to tell us the bad news. The good news is only good insofar as the bad is bad. That's why the hermeneutical principle about Scripture is so important: one should always interpret the Old Testament by the New Testament and the different parts of Scripture by the whole.

When Paul says that we are no longer under the law, he is not saying that the law is no longer relevant and true or that, in our breaking of it, God doesn't have the right to be angry. He has every right! Once you see God's power and holiness, and you know yourself, traffic with God is a very scary thing. Be afraid. Be very afraid!

They told me that if I was obedient, holy, and pure, God would be pleased and would love me. You know something? They were right. And I tried. I mean I really tried. I read and studied Scripture. I exercised all the volitional power in me to avoid the evil. I prayed a lot and worked hard at being a *good* person. I even got ordained. Then I came to the realization that no matter how hard I tried, I couldn't do it anymore.

Just when I turned and started to walk away sorrowful, he spoke. *"Welcome, child! Welcome!"* I came running and I've never left, because nobody ever loved me that way, forgave me that much, and cared for me that deeply. But without the "bad news," I never would have come.

5. Okay, but what about obedience?

I spent a lot of space in this book talking about the irrelevance of our obedience, but let me say it again, and try to listen this time. If Jesus covered all your sins on the cross, you don't have to cover them. They are already covered. Okay? If God has put the incredible goodness and obedience of Jesus Christ into your account, there's enough, and you don't have to add to it. When you try to cover your own sins (by being obedient or denying they're there) and

> *If Jesus covered all your sins on the cross, you don't have to cover them.*

be more righteous than God's own Son . . . you're like a man who wears a bra. You're weird, you may like it, but it doesn't do you any good and has no practical purpose.

Sorry.

6. Is holiness and sanctification irrelevant?

Of course not. Let me tell you how I became a spiritual giant.

Okay, not that, but at least how I got better. I tried to work at it, and I got worse. I tried to place the world behind me and the cross before me, but I kept looking back and then, on many occasions, backtracked. I tried to fill my mind with Scripture and make all sorts of promises, but my obsessive mind wouldn't let go of my sin. I broke so many promises that, like smoking my pipe and giving up quitting, I quit quitting and making promises.

I so wanted to bring gifts to God. When I told him that, he laughed and said, *"Come here, child!"* I came, and he loved me without condition. Then I noticed that I was better. I still didn't have any gifts to give him, but I did (and do) say, "Wow!" In that "Wow!" is the worship and praise that defines who I am. When I tell people that Jesus likes me 10 percent more than he likes them, it is not bragging. It's praise. I was created for that!

7. What about discipline? You very conveniently avoid Hebrews 12:7. It says, in case you don't know, "It is for discipline that you have to endure. God is treating you as sons. For what son is there whom his father does not discipline?"

The reason I don't refer to that very often is that it is the weapon of choice in the hands of the manipulators. They (and I on occasion) give the gift with one hand and take it away with the other. In other words: God loves us without condition; but if you don't respond appropriately to his love, he'll take you out to the woodshed, and you won't be able to walk for a week.

What's with that?

I can't tell you how many times I've heard people with cancer, AIDS, rebellious children, lost jobs, and a thousand other "dark" experiences refer to Hebrews 12:7. They are sure that God, in his love, is disciplining them. One time a man even told me, after he lost his family, that God was disciplining him because he stole a quarter from his mother's purse when he was twelve.

Nonsense. If there were a correlation between our obedience and his discipline, we would have been destroyed a long time ago.

This isn't a book given over to a proper exegesis of Hebrews 12:7, but it is proper to take the *father* in that passage and apply it to the Father Jesus re-

> *If there were a correlation between our obedience and his discipline, we would have been destroyed a long time ago.*

vealed. It is also quite proper to compare a *good father* to our images of a heavenly one. Jesus said, "If you then, who are evil, know how to give good gifts to your children, how much more will your Father who is in heaven give good things to those who ask him!" (Matthew 7:11).

My father was *evil* by human standards, but there was never a man who loved his sons more than my father. He was not a very good disciplinarian and was criticized for it. In fact, he only spanked me twice in all the years I was growing up. That wasn't because I only deserved to be spanked twice (are you kidding?); it was just all he could muster. And he wept real tears both times. Do you know what happened those two times? Afterward, I got hugged and I got ice cream. In fact, it was worth the spanking just to get the ice cream. The hugs too! It just took me a lot of years to see that the hugs were more important than the ice cream.

If we're going to teach discipline to God's people (and we should), it must always be done with the Father whom

Jesus revealed and my father in mind. If it isn't, it's just a back doorway to pour on the guilt and to keep God's people in line.

8. You don't seem to care much for excellence nor do you have a very high view of human nature. Don't you think you've gone a bit too far?

Are you kidding? I didn't go far enough!

My late friend, Jack Miller, founder of World Harvest Mission, used to say that the entire Bible could be summed up with two sentences: (1) Cheer up . . . you're a lot worse than you think you are, and (2) cheer up . . . God's grace is a lot bigger than you think it is.

When I first heard Jack say that, I knew it was one of those statements that changes lives. It changed mine. I got it in a profound way. Over the years subsequent to that initial hearing, I've found out that I'm a lot worse that I thought I was then and I'm a lot worse than I think I am now. I discovered that grace was not only a lot bigger than I thought it was. It's a lot bigger than I have said in this book.

9. Okay, but where do you draw the line?

There isn't one. And as soon as you draw one, it ceases to be the gospel.

My friend Zach Van Dyke, a youth pastor and a regular on our talk show, recently attended a conference for youth leaders with some three or four thousand people. One of the main speakers was Ted Haggard. He was the president of the National Association of Evangelicals and pastor of a megachurch when it was discovered, based on the claims of a male prostitute, that he was buying drugs; he later admitted to "sexual immorality."

I don't know Ted Haggard, but I have heard some of the pain he's gone through subsequent to his *fall*. Shame, financial ruin, and loss of friendships and ministry are just a part of it. I suspect his nights are very dark. But he has "come back home," and his repentance is now as notorious as his sin.

When Ted was introduced to these youth-ministry people, Zach told me that a whole lot of people (maybe as many as a thousand) stood up and walked out of the auditorium. I get that and suspect they felt they were taking a stand for Christ. Sometimes one must do that. But this time when they left the building, Jesus didn't go with them. He stayed behind and rejoiced in the "coming home" of Ted Haggard.

But that isn't the tragedy. The tragedy is that in that crowd there were some who were hesitant about whether to stay or leave because of their own failure and sin; and they remained silent, hiding their own unworthiness. Hiding and silence almost killed Ted Haggard, and it will kill them too.

No, there isn't a line.

*10. What about right and wrong? You don't seem
to care about that.*

I once spoke to the missionaries of a large mission organization, and God (believe it or not) used my words in
the lives of many of the missionaries. I did some teaching
and some confessing. They go together.

One of the missionaries who was quite angry, stood up
and said so. I was feeling like dirt when another missionary stood up and said, "You don't understand. Just because someone is honest about not meeting the standard
doesn't mean that he ignores
or lowers the standard."

> "Just because someone is
> honest about not meeting
> the standard doesn't mean
> that he ignores or lowers
> the standard."

I've thought about what
the second missionary said
ever since, and he's right.
The Ten Commandments
aren't suggestions, immoral-
ity is immoral, and our sin is destructive to us and to everybody we love. If someone is drowning in a swimming
pool, that person (unless he or she is particularly stupid)
knows that swimming is the solution. In that situation, it
seems wise for the drowning person to say (or yell in
panic), "I can't swim!" and to accept the lifeguard's help.
Just so, dealing with our sin is a serious problem and
"stopping sinning" is the solution. Problem is, we can't
stop. Then we get help (that would be Jesus), and the
swimming lessons begin. But the lessons always start and
continue with helplessness.

I still haven't learned to be an Olympic swimmer (it's important that we're honest about that lest we discourage others who can't swim), but I'm better at it than I was. And I'm even better when I remember the Lifeguard who stands watch just in case I get in trouble.

11. What about being missional? If Christians buy into what you've taught, won't people stop going on the mission field, feeding the hungry, reaching out to the poor, and caring for those in need?

In fact, just the opposite.

Someone recently gave me a coffee mug. This was written on it (a lot of writing for a small mug): "In America you are not required to offer food to the hungry or shelter to the homeless. There is no ordinance forcing you to visit the lonely or comfort the infirm. Nowhere in the Constitution does it say you have to provide clothing for the poor. In fact, one of the nicest things about living here is that you really don't have to do anything for anybody."

True enough.

Here's an interesting fact. In every major study, America is one of the most generous countries in the world (often the most generous) in terms of how much is given by private individuals to charity. I suspect there are a lot of different reasons for that, but maybe one of the major reasons is the lack of coercion.

Do-goodism watered by guilt only goes so far and lasts so long. Do-gooders grow weary and go home. After they leave, though, those who have been loved keep on loving. Those who have been forgiven keep on forgiving. Those who have been rescued stay around to rescue others.

William Booth, cofounder of the Salvation Army with his wife, Catherine, is famously quoted as having the poor of London "on his heart." Who put them there? Why did he care? Where did he get that compassion? He got it from Jesus. Hanging out with Jesus will do that to you. If you get it from guilt, it won't last; but if it does, it will end up making you self-righteous . . . so much so it would probably be better for you to just go home with all the do-gooders.

12. Aren't you a bit pessimistic about human beings?

No more than the Bible is.

I was recently interviewed by a Chicago radio station about some results garnered by George Barna in his studies of the church. I was told that Barna had discovered that the divorce rate of Christians was about the same as that of unbelievers, and that Christians were no more compassionate, socially aware, and involved in their communities than non-Christians.

The host who interviewed me probably expected me to preach about how we have left our heritage and betrayed our God. I'm fairly good at that.

Instead I said, "What did you expect? When we joined the church, we told the world we were screwed up. I'm glad George Barna found out that it wasn't a lie. But frankly, I could have saved him a lot of effort and money, and told him that beforehand."

The fact is, unbelievers are often better than Christians. They have to fake it because it's all they've got.

> When we joined the church, we told the world we were screwed up.

13. Doesn't that lead to "wormology" and a bad self-image?

Actually, no.

Let me tell you what leads to a bad self-image. Lies lead to a bad self-image. Self-esteem (in the best sense of that word) comes from being valued. At minimum, the gospel takes human beings seriously—their sin, the implications of sin, and the consequences of sin. There is great value in being taken seriously. There is even greater value in being loved anyway.

I'm often criticized for being arrogant with the additional editorial comment that there was never anybody who had less reason to be arrogant. Bingo. But my Father thinks I'm wonderful! He loves me, and in that love, my self-esteem goes through the roof and sometimes appears to be arrogance. Sorry, but I just can't help it.

14. What if you're wrong?

I'm in trouble.

You are too.

In fact, if what I've written in this book isn't true, neither of us has a prayer.

NOTES

Introduction

1. If you go to the talk show's website (SteveBrownEtc.com), you will notice that there is a place where you can email three free sins to your friends (or enemies). It is a kind of backdoor way to say something about the gospel. The statement on the page reads, "If you're a pagan, you'll have to pay for your own sins, but feel free to click on the links and enjoy Steve and his friends at no additional cost to you."

Chapter 1: The Impossible Task of Flying Frogs

1. And if you're really good at faking it, publishers will even ask you to write books on helping people to fly.

Chapter 2: How's It Working for You So Far?

1. Calvin Miller, *The Singer Trilogy* (Downer's Grove, IL: InterVarsity, 1980), 83.
2. Emile Coue, www.quotationspage.com/quotes/Emile_Coue.
3. "Advantages from Remaining Sin" (from a letter written by

John Newton, April, 1772), www.gospelweb.net/JohnNewton/
advantagesfromremainingsin.htm.

4. Henri J. M. Nouwen, *In the Name of Jesus* (New York: Crossroad, 1989), 28–30.

Chapter 3: Repent! The End Is Near!

1. Heidelberg Catechism Q & A: 60, www.crcna.org/pages/
heidelberg_spirit.cfm#QandA60.

2. *The Book of Common Prayer* (New York: Seabury, 1979), Holy Eucharist I, 331.

3. C. S. Lewis, *The Weight of Glory* (New York: HarperOne, 2001), 141.

4. Ronald Rolheiser, *The Holy Longing: The Search for a Christian Spirituality* (New York: Doubleday, 1999), 128–29.

Chapter 4: Why Can't We All Just Get Along?

1. For details, go to: http://www.gatheringnations.ca.

2. Catherine Claire Larson, *As We Forgive: Stories of Reconciliation from Rwanda* (Grand Rapids: Zondervan, 2009).

3. Larson, *As We Forgive.*

4. See the story of Achan in Joshua 7 and how sin affects a nation.

5. Martin Bucer, *Psalter with Complete Church Practice* (Strasbourg: http://anglicanprayer.wordpress.com/2010/02/17/a-lenten
-prayer-of-confession-based-on-the-decalogue/1534).

Chapter 5: Ain't Gonna Study War No More!

1. David Learn. Story originally appeared in online newsletter. Fishers of Grin.

Notes

Chapter 6: The Wuss Factor

1. Eric Metaxas, *Bonhoeffer: Pastor, Martyr, Prophet, Spy* (Nashville: Thomas Nelson, 2010), 246.
2. Nate Larken, *Samson and the Pirate Monks: Calling Men to Authentic Brotherhood* (Nashville: Thomas Nelson, 2007), 90.
3. Dick Staub, *About You* (San Francisco: Jossey-Bass, 2010), 193.
4. Wayne Terry, *Time Zones: Slipping Away* (Lee's Summit, MO: Father's Press, 2009).

Chapter 7: When Getting Better Doesn't Matter

1. David Kinnaman and Gabe Lyons, *unChristian: What a New Generation Really Thinks about Christianity . . . and Why It Matters* (Grand Rapids: Baker, 2007).
2. Jim Henderson, Todd Hunter, and Craig Spinks, *The Outsider Interviews: A New Generation Speaks Out on Christianity* (Grand Rapids: Baker, 2010).
3. C. S. Lewis, *The Weight of Glory* (Grand Rapids: Eerdmans, 1949), 57–58, 63.

Chapter 8: The Other Side of Silence

1. Blaise Pascal, *Pensees* in Great Books of the Western World Vol. 33 Pascal (Chicago: Encyclopedia Britannica, Inc., 1952), 211.

Chapter 9: The Devil Made Me Do It!

1. C. S. Lewis, *The Screwtape Letters* (New York: Harper Collins, 1942), ix.
2. Arthur Bennett, ed., *The Valley of Vision: A Collection of Puritan Prayers & Devotions* (Edinburgh: Banner of Truth Trust, 1975), 72.

Chapter 10: A Party Down at the Church

1. Tina Firesheets, "Massive dinner is all about connecting" in the Greensboro *News-Record*, February 15, 2009. www.news-record.com/content/2009/02/15/article/massive_dinner_is_all_about_connecting.
2. Philip Yancey, "A Living Stream in the Desert," *Christianity Today*, November 12, 2010. www.christianitytoday.com/ct/2010/november/20.30.html.

Chapter 11: Just Don't Let Them!

1. William D. Hendricks, *Exit Interviews: Revealing Stories of Why People Are Leaving the Church* (Chicago: Moody, 1993), 279–80.
2. Timothy F. Lull, ed., *Martin Luther's Basic Theological Writings* (Minneapolis: Fortress, 1989), 609.
3. Terry Mattingly, "What we do, why we do it," GetReligion.org, www.getreligion.org/2004/02/what-were-doing-here/.
4. Jonathan Edwards, *The Religious Affections* (Point Roberts, WA: Eremitical Press, 2009), 176.

ACKNOWLEDGMENTS

There are so many people who "hold my arms" and are gifts of God's grace . . .

My wife, Anna, and my family,

Our daughter, Robin DeMurga, with her gifted editing, hard work, and loving wisdom,

Howard Books/Simon & Schuster—my friend and senior editor, Philis Boultinghouse; associate editor, Jessica Wong; senior production editor, Jessica Chin; and their entire hard-working (and flexible!) production team,

Wolgemuth & Associates, Inc.—my agents Robert D. Wolgemuth, my longtime friend, and Erik S. Wolgemuth who is amazing,

George Bingham and the incredible, gifted staff at Key Life Network, Inc., including Cathy Wyatt (who has been with me more years than either of us would admit!), and . . .

A bunch of others . . .

. . . all of whom love me anyway, fix me, and make me and this book far better than I or it would have been.

ABOUT THE AUTHOR

DR. STEVE BROWN is a broadcaster, seminary professor, author, and the founder and president of Key Life Network. He previously served as a pastor for over twenty-five years and now devotes much of his time to the radio broadcasts *Key Life* and *Steve Brown Etc.*

Dr. Brown serves as professor emeritus of preaching at Reformed Theological Seminary. He sits on the board of the National Religious Broadcasters and Harvest USA. Traveling extensively, he is a much-in-demand speaker.

Steve is the author of numerous books, including *A Scandalous Freedom, What Was I Thinking?, When Being Good Isn't Good Enough,* and *How to Talk So People Will Listen.* His articles appear in such magazines and journals as *Relevant, Leadership, Decision, Plain Truth,* and *Today's Christian Woman.*